BARRIE MAHONEY

Barrie Mahoney worked as a teacher and head teacher in the south west of England, and then became a school inspector in England and Wales. A new life and career as a newspaper reporter in Spain's Costa Blanca led to him launching and editing an English language newspaper in the Canary Islands. Following the successful publication of his novels, 'Journeys and Jigsaws' and 'Threads and Threats', and then 'Letters from the Atlantic' and 'Expat Survival' that give an amusing and reflective view of life abroad, he is still enjoying life in the sun and writes regular columns for newspapers and magazines in Spain, Portugal, Ireland, Australia, South Africa, Canada and the USA.

Visit the author's websites:

www.barriemahoney.com

www.thecanaryislander.com

www.twittersfromtheatlantic.com

Other books by Barrie Mahoney

Journeys and Jigsaws (Vanguard Press) 2009
ISBN: 978 184386 538 4 (Paperback and Kindle)

Threads and Threats (Vanguard Press) 2011
ISBN: 978 184386 646 6) Paperback and Kindle)

Letters from the Atlantic (Vanguard Press) 2011
ISBN: 978 184386 645 9 (Paperback and Kindle)

Expat Survival (The Canary Islander Publishing) 2012
ISBN: 978 1479130481 (Paperback and Kindle)

Other publications by Barrie Mahoney

News from the Canary Islands (Kindle) 2011

Twitters from the Atlantic (Kindle) 2011

Living the Dream

BARRIE MAHONEY

The Canary Islander Publishing

© Copyright 2011

Barrie Mahoney

The right of Barrie Mahoney to be identified as author of this work has been asserted by him in accordance with the Copyright, Designs and Patents Act 1988.

All Rights Reserved

No reproduction, copy or transmission of this publication may be made without written permission. No paragraph of this publication may be reproduced, copied or transmitted save with the written permission of the author, or in accordance with the provisions of the Copyright Act 1956 (as amended). Any person who commits any unauthorised act in relation to this publication may be liable to criminal prosecution and civil claims for damages.

A CIP catalogue record for this title is available from the British Library.

ISBN 9781461029090

www.barriemahoney.com

First Published in 2011
The Canary Islander Publishing

The
Canary
Islander

DEDICATION

*To my life partner, David, for his love and support
and for travelling the journey together.*

The Canary Islander

Acknowledgements

I would like to thank all those people that I have met on my journey to where I am now.

To supportive friends who helped me to overcome the many problems and frustrations that I faced and taught me much about learning to adapt to a new culture. Also, to friends in the UK, or scattered around the world, who kept in touch despite being so far away.

To people that I met through working as a newspaper reporter and editor in Spain and the Canary Islands and the privilege of sharing their successes and challenges in life.

LIVING THE DREAM

CONTENTS

Preface – It began with a dream   16

Living the Dream   24

Airports and Travel   27

A Bit of a Wrench   28
A Pair of Shorts and a Toothbrush   32
Holiday Souvenirs   36
Airport Security   39
What Does a Scotsman Wear Beneath His Kilt?   42

Post, Phone and Email   45

A Drag Queen at the Correos   46
Keeping in Touch   49
"Lots of Love" or "Laugh Out Loud"?   52
Postal Express?   55
Tomorrow, Tomorrow...!   58

Food and Drink   61

A Recession Busting Breakfast   62
Marmite Soldier, Anyone?   65
Tortillas Are Not Always What They Seem   67
A Drop of the Hard Stuff   70

Environmental 73

Saving the Planet with a Plastic Bag	74
Scotch and Oestrogen, Sir?	77
The Canarian Calima	80
The Magic Blue Ball	83
The Week the Planes Stopped Flying	86
Water from Wind	90
Cars from Bananas	93
Seaside Burps	96

Language and Culture 99

Fax Machines and Bureaucrats	100
Love thy Neighbour - Canaries style	103
The Sunday Slowdown	106
'The Big Sleep'	109
The End of The Siesta?	112
The Spanish Mistress and the Gym Master	114
Not Exactly Cool...!	117

Historical 119

Greenwich Mean Time and the Canary Islands	120
World War Heroes	123
The Virgin and the Pines	126

Health 128

The Boob Job	129
A Playground for the Wrinklies	132
A Question of Convenience (Health)	135
"We Love The NHS!"	138

Legal and Financial 141

Whack a Banker!	142
Until Death Do Us Part (or until someone better comes along)	145
The Telemarketing Plague	149
The Parking Ticket	152
Police Crackdown on Speeding Infants	155

Attitudes 158

Build 'Em Up and Knock 'Em Down	159
The UK Election and the Euro Brit	162
The Beautiful Game?	165
Fancy a Change of Career?	168
Boot-camps, (Arch)Bishops and Blogs	171

People, Pets and Places 173

'From Teacher to Drag Queen'	174
A Canarian Garden	176
Walking the Dog	179
A Cat and Dog Story	182
The Uniqueness of Gran Canaria	185

Disclaimer

This is a book about real people, real places and real events, but names of people and companies have been changed to avoid any embarrassment.

Preface

It began with a dream

When we sleep we sometimes have dreams that come and go in our unconscious state; some dreams are just a little bit of nonsense, whilst others stay with us. Sometimes these dreams become something new for us to achieve or maybe to do something different or better. Maybe it is a dream of a better life, more money, less pressure at work, sunshine, beaches, blue skies, mountains, lakes, quiet places and noisy and exciting places. Dreams are unique, yet there are themes in dreams that bring many people with a common interest together.

For me the dream has often been about islands. From a small boy seeing Brownsea Island in Poole Harbour for the very first time, I have always wanted to live on one. Maybe it would be the Isle of Wight, the Scilly Islands, the Isle of Skye or maybe even further afield?

Maybe the dream will lead to living in another country, working in a different culture, meeting new people, learning more about the world, widening horizons, improving future job prospects, making more money, making new friends and probably learning a new language. For many, the thought of moving to live for a time or forever in another country may remain a dream or a fantasy; a plan for next year, when the kids grow up, after retirement or when there is a big win on the lottery. However, many others actually do live their dream. So how do they live the dream? What did they do? Were they just lucky? Can only some people live their dream?

Another climate will not appeal to all dreamers, as many enjoy the patterns of seasonal weather. The cycle of spring signalling the beginnings of new life and also signalling the end of the cold, wet, winter weather, also has a spiritual uplift for many people around the world. Summer for most people brings time for holidays or more time for relaxation and outdoor activities that can be so miserable in winter weather conditions. Of course, this all depends where you live in the world, as some countries see greater differences in seasons than others, but the security of weather patterns becomes part of growing up and living and who we are.

Despite feelings of contentment with seasons, many

people just want to live in a climate where it is not too cold or too wet, and where it is possible to swim in the sea without freezing or to lie on a sun terrace with a cool glass of wine. People who move abroad for a better climate are often called expats and will certainly be foreigners in another country, but they are not lucky or different. They just decided to live their dream, maybe for just part of the year or maybe to stay for longer. If they were not just lucky, what did they do to achieve this? How can we live our dreams?

Another lifestyle will appeal when the pressures of money, families, relationships, jobs and pressure to conform to society's expectations of what people should do and how to behave become too much to bear. Many people will have a lifestyle with which they are content and happy, and can cope easily with the ups and downs of life; the rollercoaster ride that at times takes your breath away and at other times threatens your sanity and stability.

Society expects people to fit in, but there are many people who simply cannot for many reasons, and often for reasons that they cannot explain to others or perhaps even to themselves. So moving somewhere new to follow a different lifestyle is very appealing, especially if the new lifestyle gives less personal pressure, a job without unrealistic demands, a different type of relationship, breathing space away from claustrophobic families, to earn more money or maybe to live where the cost of living is lower. How about a new lifestyle? How did others achieve a better lifestyle? Can I live my dream?

I have learned many things in life, but one lesson that I learned many years ago was that whatever you plan it will change and be better or worse than the original plan; however, it will be different. Life experiences are sometimes good, but they can also be sad, threatening, unhappy and very dark. However, a dream remains with you throughout your life; it starts as a want and then becomes a need. So, to live your dream you need to believe in the dream, and begin to open a new chapter in your life; this chapter is blank yet you are going to write it.

I grew up in a rural part of Lincolnshire in the UK and then moved to a large town on the south coast to work as a civil servant, and then a new chapter opened and I trained to be a teacher, and eventually became a head teacher of two schools. Throughout this time I had a dream to live on an island, and spent many holidays exploring different islands around the UK and Europe. Only one island offered the perfect appeal for me, but it was not in the UK, and is the subject of another book.

For me life is like a jigsaw, with me trying to fit pieces into spaces that do not always seem to be right. The easiest part of a jigsaw is seeing the final picture that you have made, but the jigsaw of life only becomes clear when we near the end of our lives; maybe just a little late! Journeys are also an important part of our lives as we travel to school, to work, to other places for work or holidays, or just travelling through life; learning and growing from our achievements, as well as from our mistakes. Journeys and Jigsaws became part of the dream of finding this elusive island, but I could not explain what directions the journey would take or how the parts could fit into the jigsaw, but 'Journeys and Jigsaws' did become part of fulfilling the dream as the title for my first novel.

A new direction began when I became a school inspector for schools in England and Wales, and made many journeys to visit some amazing and wonderful schools where teachers were educating young children and giving them dreams for their future. This job was a privilege and a wonderful experience, but I always believed that we need to know our own sell-by-date, and I sensed that my own was approaching. So it was time to move on, but where?

My move from the UK to the Costa Blanca in Spain and then the Canary Islands in the middle of the Atlantic and just off the west coast of Africa led me to experience incidents that were hilarious, frustrating, unbelievable and heart warming. These reflections (or Twitters as I call them in my magazine and newspaper columns) are about living as an expat or foreigner in another country, and I am happy to share these with the reader if, like me, you have a desire to live the dream and want to learn more from those that have begun to write a new chapter in their lives.

This book is meant to entertain and amuse, as well as to encourage and support you to live your dream - whatever and wherever that is!

What was the name of the island where I had

wanted to live so many years ago? It was Gran Canaria.

Living the Dream

Living the Dream

When I moved to the Costa Blanca, I recall being told by one consular official that, "The Brits come here to die". I quickly discovered that nothing could be further from the truth. In my newly appointed role as a newspaper reporter, I quickly realised that far from going to the Costa Blanca to die, the Brits and other expats had moved to the Costa Blanca to live - and a very good job they were making of it too!

Many people that I met had finally been released from the crippling pain of arthritis and other conditions linked to a cold, damp Northern European climate and had quickly realised that a whole new world of mobility was waiting for them. Others had realised their dream of a home in the sun, inspired by the many "You can do it too" TV programmes, earlier in life - thanks to rising house prices and the newly found equity that they had discovered in their homes. All had one thing in common, fulfilling the dream of a new life and adventure in the sun.

I quickly discovered tap dancing groups, where it was not unusual to discover ninety-year-olds treading the boards, orchestral groups and brass bands, salsa classes, walking groups and drama groups. The area was buzzing with activity and it always amazed and delighted me to see so many British, Scandinavian, German, Irish and Spanish, as well as many other nationalities, enjoying being together. One thing that united many expats was the desire to see a rapid improvement in animal welfare, and I am convinced that the present level of animal welfare in the Costas, although still not ideal, is due to the efforts of the many expat groups, working alongside their Spanish counterparts.

Now that I am living in the Canary Islands there is, of course, a much smaller expat population. The climate is such that much of the expat social life revolves around the bar culture. There are few activities that expats are involved in, although there are plenty of Canarian music, drama and cultural groups to be found, but the enthusiasm for joining these is less obvious than in the Costas. There is also a much younger expat population living on the islands, whose main focus is earning a living and paying the rent or the mortgage. This does not leave a great deal of time for other activities in an area where wages are low and unemployment is high.

Sadly, some expats do not succeed in their attempts to create a new life in the sun. For many, 'living the dream' rapidly becomes 'living the nightmare'. Illness, relationship problems, bereavement or unemployment drives many to return 'home' disillusioned, but wiser. In time, I hope that these would-be expats realise that no experience in life is ever wasted, and that the broader experiences that they will have gained, will stand them in good stead for the future, whatever they choose to do.

Some time ago, I met someone who was well versed in spiritual matters, and commented that ancient ley lines intersect these islands. As a result, these islands draw in a certain kind of person and let go of those it does not want. I remember him commenting that these islands have a force that cannot be avoided. I was sceptical at first, but I have noticed over the years that I have lived here, that of the many would-be expats who have arrived and returned disillusioned, a significant number of these have returned to the islands again a few years later and settled successfully. Many will say that this is due to a positive change in personal circumstances, and a desire to seek the sun and warmth once again. However, maybe, just maybe, the islands have drawn them back again?

Airports and Travel

A Bit of a Wrench

Airports give me problems. Whether it is excess luggage or simply that the wretched security alarms will just not stop bleeping when I enter their territory; it is always an annoying and often embarrassing experience. My recent visit to the UK was a case in point.

Some time ago I was tempted to purchase a new kind of adjustable spanner. It was marketed heavily on television and in the national press and after a sorry incident with our downstairs loo - I won't go into detail here - and many hours of grappling with all manner of antiquated tools, I decided that if I had one of these new 'super spanners' the job would have been done in a flash. Although I dropped many hints to my partner, sadly one did not appear in my Christmas stocking.

After Christmas none were to be seen in the shops and it was my brother who came to the rescue. He would order one from Amazon and give it to me when I returned to the UK. Why he could not have had it sent direct to me I did not like to ask and so I looked forward to collecting the magic tool during my next visit to see the family.

"Now then sir, is this your bag?" came an officious sounding voice at Gatwick Airport security. I had just been frisked once again by a security officer and had thought that my ordeal was over for the time being. I nodded.

"Would you mind coming over to this table whilst I empty your bag? We have just x-rayed your bag and you have two suspicious items inside. I would like to examine these items more closely and in your presence." I was beckoned to a nearby table whilst the security officer donned rubber gloves and began removing all the items from my bag. Oh dear, here we go again!

"My, sir certainly likes his toys, doesn't he?" frowned the security officer as he removed a laptop computer, three mobile phones, various adapters, Tom Tom navigation unit and accessories as well as a number of cables, dongles and plug ins. He frowned again as he retrieved a number of small Christmas presents carefully packed by an elderly relative. He waved one of the small items in the air. "This is one of them. Do you know what's inside?"

I had no idea, but suddenly realising that this was not the correct answer, I replied, "A potato peeler. I cannot get a good one at home and Auntie Gertie thought we would like it."

The security officer smiled. "Hmm, yes, it feels like it. It would be a pity to open it, wouldn't it? Would spoil Auntie Gertie's surprise. I'll x-ray it again and see." This time he was being remarkably helpful and I thanked him. After a moment or two he returned to the table with a spring in his step.

"Yes, that's it. A potato peeler it is, but don't tell Auntie Gertie I told you." He laughed heartily. "Now what about this other item?"

The security officer proceeded to remove the last items from my large and heavy bag. "Hmm, now if I am not mistaken, I think you will find that this is the problem." He triumphantly held my brother's gift - my new adjustable spanner in the air. "You cannot take this on board, sir. This wrench is potentially a dangerous weapon."

"You cannot be serious," I responded angrily. "It is not a wrench, it is an adjustable spanner," I protested, but sensibly recognising that a dialogue about the Oxford Dictionary definition of both spanner and a wrench would not be entirely appropriate at this point. "Look it is still in its plastic packaging. You would need a strong pair of scissors, if not a sharp knife, to open it. We all know that any self respecting terrorist would only consider carrying out his dastardly deed with a pair of nail scissors or a nail file, but I cannot see any terrorist wanting to use my spanner without first removing it from its plastic packaging. To do that they would need scissors or a sharp knife which, as we both know, are banned," I added triumphantly.

This was the wrong response and for a moment I thought that I was about to be arrested. The security officer frowned. "This item, sir, is a dangerous wrench and in the wrong hands it could be a lethal weapon just as it is, plastic packaging and all. I have no alternative, but to confiscate it. You will just have to tell your Auntie Gertie that we are sorry, but she really must not send you back on flights with dangerous items in your hand luggage."

Dear Auntie Gertie, who died long ago I might add, would be spinning in her grave if she knew that an innocent potato peeler and an adjustable spanner, attributed to her generosity in the spur of the moment, were considered even possible threats for an act of terrorism. Now her heavy handbag and sharp stiletto heels were an entirely different matter... Sorry, Auntie!

A Pair of Shorts and a Toothbrush

As much as I love visiting friends and family in the UK and Ireland, the necessary air flight fills me with dread, which is why I avoid this tortuous ordeal as much as possible. No, it is not the actual flying part, nor the possibility of catching pig flu from all that recycled air, nor being crammed into airport buses and queues and not even the major airports' policy of processing passengers like sardines. No, my horrors begin when packing my suitcase, or several in my case, a week or so before the trip. Recent luggage restrictions are ridiculous, after all, my wash-bag alone is almost the entire weight allowance. Add to that, two shirts a day for 14 days, all the necessary vests and thermal underwear, gloves, scarves and hot water bottles - all so essential for a trip away from home, as well as a more than generous inclusion of essential gadgets and their necessary chargers and adapters and you will understand the pain, suffering and soul searching that I have to endure. Yes, I know, I am not alone in my whinging and I do fully understand all about global warming - as if an extra shirt or two would make any difference...!

A very good friend of mine recently took me in hand after I had explained the distress of my forthcoming situation. I listened carefully as he, in whispered tones, revealed some of his travel tips. He laughed, rather cruelly I thought, when he heard of the number of shirts and socks that I had planned to take. "You will be wearing vests, so take just three shirts. Make each one last for two days and then go to the launderette," he laughed. He passed on other gems too - all equally drastic measures.

Hmm, and a good dose of deodorant, I thought to myself, but not wishing to appear ungrateful I continued to listen to his pearls of wisdom. After all, my friend was an ex-marine who had travelled throughout Laos, Thailand and Vietnam for several months with little more than a pair of shorts and a toothbrush. He taught me how to roll and not to fold my clothes. Did I really need to take an electric shaver, electric toothbrush, hairdryer and iron? He thought not and I, after several stiff brandies, eventually agreed, albeit reluctantly.

The big day arrived and I tentatively balanced my suitcase in my partner's hands as he balanced on the scales. After the deduction of his weight and a few adjustments I smugly realised that the overall weight of the proposed luggage was now just 16 kilograms! That was indeed a record for me and I set off to the airport with a new air of confidence, knowing that I had four kilograms available for newly purchased goodies!

Two weeks later I was standing at the dreaded Gatwick airport, queuing to have my bags checked. I had suffered two weeks of just three shirts, visited the launderette twice, had plenty of showers and used lots of deodorant. No one had commented about my wearing the same items of clothing for two weeks and I stood with confidence in the queue waiting my turn. Certainly I had bought a few things, collected the usual batch of Christmas presents from generous relatives. I had bought two large bottles of Vitamin C tablets as well - have you noticed the acute shortage on the islands?

"Had a good trip, sir," came a friendly voice from a spotty youth wearing a smart uniform. This chirpiness took me back a little as both age and experience has taught me that such chirpiness from anyone official in airports throughout the world usually means trouble.

"You're a little overweight, sir," continued The Spotty Charmer, grinning broadly. I thought he could have chosen his phrasing a little more carefully. After all I have been wasting away on a diet for three months or so.

"How much overweight?" I snapped coldly, not about to indulge in pleasantries.

"Ten kilograms, sir. You must have bought a lot of stuff in the UK. I hope it's worth it because that little lot will cost you £100." The Spotty Charmer had suddenly become officious and demanding in his voice, but he continued to smile broadly, although the breadth of the smile was thankfully restricted by the brace on his teeth.

"That's impossible," I replied. "Anyway, ten kilograms at £5 per kilogram is only £50. You are trying to overcharge me, young man."

"Not so, sir. If you pre-book your excess luggage before your flight then you can have it for £5 per kilo. If not, it is £10, sir." I no longer liked the way he referred to me as "sir". It had an evil resonance about it.

"What rubbish," I spluttered. "How can I possibly foresee what the overall weight of my luggage will be until I have completed my trip. How can I judge that beforehand?"

"Well, that is your problem sir. Will sir be taking anything out of his case or will sir be paying by credit card?"

"This is preposterous," I exploded. "Sir will certainly not be taking anything out of his case," I retorted proffering my well-used credit card.

"That'll do nicely," beamed The Spotty Charmer, whisking the card out of my hand and into his evil machine.

I sighed, knowing when I was beaten. How my friend had travelled the length and breadth of Asia with a pair of shorts and a toothbrush I shall never know!

Holiday souvenirs

For those of us who live in the Canary Islands, we already know how fortunate we are as these islands have a great deal to offer residents and tourists alike. However, sometimes visitors may get a little more than they bargained for.

At the end of our holidays many of us often like to take home a souvenir of the places that we have visited, either for relatives and friends or as a happy holiday reminder for ourselves. As for which gift to take home from the Canary Islands, I find that locally produced rum generally goes down well or maybe some of the many items produced from the local weed - the medicinal aloe vera plant. Personally, I have learned to steer clear from the dreaded turrón (a strange tasting nougat) commonly disguised as a Christmas 'treat'. Yes, I know that Canarians and Spanish are said to love the stuff, but has anyone actually ever seen a local buy a bar, let alone eat it? I think it is a sinister plot to offload as much of the foul tasting stuff as we can onto unsuspecting tourists. Now what about taking home a nice plant instead?

The first thing to say about this one is that plants are not allowed into the UK without an approved licence. Do please check the rules carefully on this one otherwise you may get rather more than you bargained for. Even so, I do know that many holidaymakers purchase cactus and other plants to take back home. After all, what could be better than a really sharp, vicious looking cactus as a treat for your least-favourite aunt? Maybe give her a packet of turrón as well for good measure. I know from experience that it works wonders with false teeth and should keep her quiet for an hour or two!

So what about the odd termite or two as pets? The UK press recently carried a report from scientists saying that Britain's only colony of termites has survived 12 years of attempts to wipe it out using chemicals. These determined little beasts, which can destroy a house by eating it, were thought to have been destroyed after an expensive eradication programme.

So what has this to do with your holiday in the Canary Islands I hear you asking? Sadly, these wood-devouring mini-beasts were discovered in 1998 in two adjoining homes at Saunton in North Devon. Scientists now believe they had been brought to the UK from the Canary Islands in a plant pot.

Since their discovery, a £190,000 eradication programme, funded by the UK Government, has tried to wipe out the colony of these determined little visitors using a variety of chemical weapons. Under the programme, the area within a 500 metre radius of the two houses was monitored, and an "insect growth regulator" called hexaflumuron was supposed to prevent the insects maturing so they would be unable to reproduce.

They were thought to have been destroyed, but the latest survey of the site has found evidence of new infestation. The scientists and exterminators have gone back to the drawing board to discover a new way of finally eradicating these unwelcome foreign visitors, although rumour has it that they are now claiming political asylum and wish to live in peace in the UK.

So if your holiday is drawing to an end, may I suggest that you hurry along to the shops and purchase some of our wonderful locally produced rum and please don't forget to take home as many packets of turrón as you can carry! We need to get rid of this foul concoction one way or another!

Airport Security

One of the many additional hassles of returning to the UK, even for a fleeting visit, are the security checks. Yes, I know that these checks are essential to thwart the potential terrorist who intends to attack a plane armed with little more than nail scissors and baby teething gel. However, I do wonder why it is me that is nearly always frisked. I can see the security officers 'eyeing me up' as I enter the 'control zone' and I have yet to discover whether it is because I look shifty or whether they just find me irresistible in some way and cannot wait to get their hands on me! Anyway, whatever the reason, I do find it mildly annoying, although often entertaining, and I just hope that they warm their hands first and get it over with as quickly as possible.

This time I approached the Gatwick security zone with supreme confidence. Yes, I had remembered to remove my watch, removed loose change and keys from my pocket, removed my belt (is this really necessary?) and checked for surprise eye piercings, nose studs or anything else that I might have overlooked and that just might set off their sensitive security system.

It was all to no avail because as I walked through the magic electronic archway a piecing alarm sounded and I was duly stopped in my tracks, firmly yet politely, by a burly, but not unattractive, security officer.

"Now what are you hiding in there?" he began pleasantly, whilst I resisted the temptation to refer to a Kalashnikov hidden in my Marks and Spencer's underwear. Yes, I know that such comments are unnecessary and potentially dangerous, but nevertheless I suddenly had an urge similar to that experienced by many - that of pulling the communication cord on the Orient Express or maybe the 16.45 from King's Cross. I smiled benignly and said nothing.

"Well, we'll just give you a quick once over, sir," he grinned, prodding me with a large instrument and waving it around my body like a magic wand. The alarm bleeped again. The security officer looked puzzled. He then discovered my mobile phone in a side pocket, which I duly removed both humbly and apologetically.

"Never mind, sir. It happens," he said pleasantly, waving his magic wand around me once more. "I see you have an iPhone, they are great gadgets, aren't they?" The alarm bleeped once again.

"Now then, sir. You having games with me? Keys? Cash, any hidden piercings that I should know about?" I didn't like the way that he said "hidden", with a smirk, and I shook my head wincing at the very thought of a Prince Albert, although I did wonder how one would get through security if one actually did have this rather painful addition to the natural order. The security officer once again waved his weapon around my body furiously, but sadly I still bleeped. This was it; I was about to be strip-searched.

"Hmm," he looked puzzled. "Maybe it is your trousers." He rubbed his hands up and down my trousers once again. "Yes, I can see a couple of small studs on the pockets, maybe that is the problem." He prodded me firmly rather like a farmer does to a bullock before sending the poor creature off to the butcher. "Yes, I am sure that is it. I think I can let you go."

I heaved a sigh of relief and thanked the security officer profusely after, not for the first time, imagining that I would be taken off to some nearby room and inspected closely with the aid of rubber gloves. I shuddered at the thought although no doubt it depends upon exactly who is officiating.

"Next time, I'll have all your clothes off," he grinned. Once again I was speechless, but made up my mind that the next time I was in Gatwick Airport I would ensure that I was wearing a new pair of Calvin Kleins and not Marks and Spencer's thermal underwear!

What Does a Scotsman Wear Beneath His Kilt?

It was another windy day at the airport. Nothing, particularly unusual in that, Canarian residents might say. After all, it is the continuous gentle breezes that make Gran Canaria such an idyllic place to live. Without these breezes, the island would be far too hot a place to live, let alone to work, during the summer months.

If you are an expat, you will possibly recognise that much of our lives tends to focus around the airport. Collecting friends and family from the airport is always a great delight, although returning them is often a very different matter. At other times, for me, regular visits to the airport are necessary to collect letters and parcels, as well as to have coffee in one of the rather good coffee shops in the airport.

I am often entertained by the antics of visitors arriving and leaving the island, and a few minutes watching returning holiday-makers in those endless queues at the Thomas Cook or Thomson check-in desks often brings its own rich rewards! I am continually amazed by the way in which those calm tour representatives mostly manage to keep their tempers under control! Recently however, my attention was drawn to the check-in desk for the flight to Morocco. It was, as usual, full of chattering men and women many of whom were dressed in elegant robes. Again, as usual, they were surrounded by massive boxes containing television sets, refrigerators, microwave ovens and washing machines. Certainly it is clear that they have a more generous baggage allowance than most of us are given for flights to the UK.

My eyes fell upon an elegant middle aged man dressed in a brilliant white robe edged with gold braiding (a jellaba). It looked splendid and, in many ways, reminded me of a bride-to-be - apart from the greying hair and beard, that is! This gentleman was clearly bored and being accompanied by several other men, who looked as if they were servants or aides, strode away from his collection of boxes and headed towards the door of the airport. He rummaged inside his splendid robe, no doubt in order to locate a packet of cigarettes or his mobile phone, and lo and behold an enormous gust of wind swept around him and lifted this gentleman's robes high above him!

Initially the gentleman looked a little embarrassed, but regaining his usual regal serenity managed to pull the offending garment once more fully around him and immediately headed for the safety of the inside of the airport - the need for a smoke now forgotten for the time being. I can now reveal the answer to the question that I am sure you have been wondering. What was he wearing beneath his glamorous robe?

Pantaloons! The gentleman was wearing baggy, flowing, purple pantaloons that looked remarkably similar to those worn by Aladdin in the pantomime, cartoon and story books. They also looked very much like a pair of curtains that I remember my Aunt Gertie having in her dining room...

So, what of the Scotsman and the kilt? Sorry, actually it was just a ruse to get you to read beneath the title! After all, 'What does a Moroccan wear beneath his jellaba?' sounds nowhere near as interesting as 'What Does a Scotsman wear beneath his kilt' does it?

Post, Phone and Email

A Drag Queen at the Correos

Like so many ex-pats living in the Canary Islands and Spain, I love receiving post from home. Be it a letter or postcard from friends or family, or maybe the occasional magazine; it is good to know that we have not been forgotten. Although there is no shortage of quality shopping opportunities in the Canary Islands, I am a strong supporter of the delights of Amazon and the QVC Shopping Channel and I am often tempted to order the occasional book, DVD or latest gadget on-line.

The world's market place really opened up when I discovered the wonders of eBay some years ago. Now, I can find almost anything on the pages of this wonderful creation. Items ranging from long obsolete batteries for my minidisc (yes, I adore iPods but somehow they never seem to meet the genius of minidisc), replacement parts for an ancient, but much loved Russell Hobbs coffee percolator to very cheap yet effective mosquito netting all find themselves winging their way to one of these tiny islands in the Atlantic.

I have to say that, in the main, the Correos postal service has been very good and I am pleased to report that everything that I have ordered has safely arrived either at our home in the Costa Blanca or the Canary Islands - eventually. However, there was very nearly one rather nasty exception.

Several weeks ago I ordered a rather splendid electronic item from Amazon - I won't bore you with all the details now, but enough to say that it was sufficiently exciting to have me waiting expectantly for the postman each day for nearly five weeks! Amazon told me confidently that delivery would take somewhere between three and seven days. Yes, that did seem a little optimistic, but we often receive post from home that has taken only three days to get to Gran Canaria. Anyway, this item was travelling by courtesy of Deutsche Post and if I know anything about our German friends, it is that an efficient postal service is one of the major assets of their country. I waited with hope and expectation...

Three weeks later the parcel had still not arrived and by the end of the fourth week I was becoming anxious and contacted Amazon. Their advice was to give it "another week" and so, once again, the anguish of waiting for the postman each morning was to be repeated.

Just as we were entering the fifth week and I had all but given up any hope of receiving it, there was a buzz on the door bell and a new, very cheery, postman was holding out a box for me! Yes, it was the long expected parcel from Amazon.

"Are you new to the job?" I asked the young postman, accusingly.

Yes, it turned out that our new postman had just been appointed. I asked what had happened to our previous postman - a very nice man who was also a part-time drag queen by night. Maybe he had deserted his postal deliveries permanently in favour of the bright lights and a wardrobe of new frocks, wigs and feather boas?

The young postman shook his head. No, it turned out that some three weeks earlier our normally reliable postman, and part time drag queen, had chopped off his middle finger during a rather nasty incident with a set of ancient curling tongs, a jar of cocktail cherries and a machete - no, please don't ask me for the gory details! As a result he could no longer continue with his postal round and it had subsequently taken Correos three weeks to appoint his replacement. Ah, so that was the reason why my parcel from Amazon was delayed. How very inconsiderate!

Keeping in Touch

Are you good at keeping in touch with the folks back home? I mean to, but somehow other things just seem to get in the way and time goes so quickly over here. Thank goodness for electronic communication. A quick call or message now and again says it all, or does it?

How do you keep in touch with the folks back home? Email, text messages, telephone, Twitter, Facebook and Skype maybe? I wonder how many of us actually write letters to our loved ones and friends nowadays?

Old habits die hard and, as an ex-teacher, I find it hard to resist reading the results of current educational research. One recent survey of 1200 seven- to fourteen-year-olds conducted for the children's charity, World Vision, surprised me. The survey discovered that one in five children had never received a handwritten letter. A quarter of children surveyed had not written a letter in the last year and 43% had not received one.

With all of us increasingly relying on email and social networking sites to communicate, the research found that a tenth of children had never written a letter themselves. Teachers and experts said that they feared young people were missing out on the pleasures and developmental benefits of letter writing. Maybe they are just over-reacting and creating a news story?

However, if we think about it, handwritten letters do seem much more personal than electronic communication. Maybe it is because by going to the trouble of physically committing words to paper, going to the post office to buy a stamp and posting a letter. Yes, I do know that queuing for a stamp at the Correos in Spain can push us towards breaking point! However, when we write a letter to someone we care about we show our investment of time and effort in a relationship. I guess that is why we tend to hang on to personal letters as keepsakes. I still have some letters written to me as a child by my grandfather and my favourite aunt.

The child gains too. The very effort of writing is a real one. Painstakingly manoeuvring the pencil or pen across the page, thinking of the best words to convey a message, and struggling with spelling and punctuation. Maybe it is an effort worth making, because it is only through practice that we become truly literate – and the experts tell us that literacy is the hallmark of human civilisation. Now, there's a really big thought for us to ponder over our gin and tonics!

So what has happened to all those letters from grandparents that I certainly remember? A letter at Christmas or birthday would often include the added bonus of a postal order too. Do you remember the excitement of opening those? Perhaps the letter even had one of the new definitive stamps stuck on if we were really lucky. Such simple pleasures!

The experts say that if we care about real relationships, we should invest in real communication, not just the quick fix of a greetings card, text or email. Hmm, maybe just for today I'm going to put away my beloved Mac laptop and write real letters to my nephews and nieces. Ah, would that mean a morning queuing at the Correos? Well, maybe not today.

"Lots of Love" or "Laugh Out Loud"?

Forget learning to speak Spanish! It is Textonyms or Textese, also known as SMS language, chatspeak, texting language or txt talk, that we should really be learning as the new language in our newly adopted country.

It all used to be so beautifully simple. In the old days it was rather easy. As a schoolboy, if one was feeling particularly lovesick, passionate or saucy we would blush deeply and include something like SWALK ("Sealed With A Loving Kiss) on the back of the envelope containing our illicit message and wicked intentions. Indeed if one was feeling especially naughty, or totally outrageous, we would write 'BURMA' on the back of the envelope. ("Be Undressed and Ready My Angel"). Straightforward and to the point, wasn't it? We all knew where we were and there would be no misunderstandings, right?

Goodness knows what the jargon of today really means. I love to receive text messages, and particularly those from one of my friends in the UK, but I have to confess that I rarely understand them. Although a perfectly competent speller in real life, the dear boy suddenly seems to enter a world of total linguistic incompetence, nay insanity, when sending text messages to me. It is not only that they read as total nonsense, but also they don't seem to save on many words or letters. In any case, do mobile phone companies really charge for the number of letters that are sent nowadays or is it that we all need an excuse to reduce the English language to the barest of bare bones in order to communicate effectively on these modern devices?

I have, in the past, been very pleasantly surprised to receive messages from texters and emailers ending with LOL, which I had assumed was a term of endearment, if not affection, meaning lots of love - endless affection that, if you think about it, is rather nice. These are very pleasant to receive and make one realise that the world isn't such a bad place after all. However, my naive bubble has at last burst and I can confess that I have been saddened to discover that these promises of endless, unending affection are not what they seem. Actually, it means "laugh out loud" or "loads of laughs", which I don't find at all amusing. It is highly disappointing to at last face the reality that all my friendly texters didn't actually love me after all.

Yes, I know that anyone over the age of 40 is now regarded as a boring old fart with one foot in the grave, but my plea is that I do try. I do understand 'gr8' means "great", 'ru' means "are you?" and that 'cryn' means "crying", but why not crayon? See my problem? In my youth we often used to use the expression 'TTFN' - maybe following the expressions of some comedian of the day, I cannot remember whom, which meant, quite simply, "Ta, ta for now", simple eh? Nowadays, modern texters even use a combination of jumbled letters in their text messages which are little more than secret code that would have made the secret agents very proud. So if they say 'ttyl, lol' they probably mean "talk to you later, lots of love" not "talk to you later, laugh out loud"; and if someone says "omg, lol" they probably mean "oh my god, laugh out loud" not "oh my god, lots of love". Are you confused as well?

It seems that for words that have no common abbreviation, texters simply remove the vowels from a word, and the reader is forced to interpret a string of consonants by adding the vowels when they receive the message. So "dictionary" becomes "dctnry", or "keyboard" becomes "kybrd". It is up to the frustrated reader to interpret the abbreviated words within the context in which it is used.

Yes, I know that language develops and grows and that it is natural for children and young people to play with and adapt language for their own use. We all did it, except that we didn't send text messages, just verbal abuse, which was so much pleasanter. Context is the clue to all this business of trying to read and interpret txtese, and is probably the reason why I shall do my best never to use it. Just imagine the problems that we could get ourselves into! BBFN (bye, bye for now)!

Postal Express?

I know from my previous work as a reporter that many expats quickly become frustrated by the antics of some of the state monopolies in Spain. Dealings with the Town Halls, water and electricity companies, Correos and Telefonica - to name a few, can become incredibly frustrating experiences and can be the stuff of nightmares. With most of these companies, I still get the feeling that they think that we are here for their benefit and not the other way around. The situation is very similar to that in the UK 15 to 20 years ago, when the then UK monopolies maintained a similar arrogance towards their customers.

My problem began several weeks ago when a Spanish friend in Alicante decided that he would like my old laptop computer. I thought I would give Correos another try, particularly as they offered a two-day Postal Express service to Peninsular Spain. It cost 24 euros - not bad in view of the size and weight of the package, and with a guaranteed two-day delivery from Las Palmas to Alicante...

Three days later I received an anxious call from my friend. No, the package had not arrived. My friend was particularly concerned because he had just called Correos in Alicante and they had told him that the package was still in Madrid.

Several days later, I received another call from my friend. He had just received a letter from the

Aduana (Customs) to say that they were holding the package in Madrid. There was tax to pay and he had to complete a form and return it to them. My friend challenged this assertion, pointing out that the package was being sent from one part of Spain to another, but this logic does not enter the world of the Aduana.

The laptop was worth only about 100 euros at best because it was several years old. Apparently, because I had purchased the laptop in the Canary Islands (and had only paid 5% IGIC tax on it when it was new), if it was sent to the Peninsular the taxman would want to claim additional tax because the Canary Islands are seen as being outside the EU and Spain for tax purposes. At this point my friend and I wondered whether it really was worth paying tax on the item. We agreed that when it was delivered, and if the tax was too high, he would reject the package and it would eventually be returned to me.

One week later, the Postal Express package had still not arrived. My friend was due to go away on holiday two days later and there would be no one at his home to receive the package. He complained to Correos in Alicante and they agreed that the package would be dispatched that same day and would arrive the following day. Needless to say, it did not arrive as promised.

Two days later, just my friend was preparing to leave for the airport, the package arrived, together with a demand for 25 euros tax. He paid up and went on holiday. The time that the package had taken to get from the Canary Islands to my friend's home in Alicante was just over two weeks - not exactly within two days as promised in the Correos advertising and, indeed, guaranteed in their terms of service.

Yet again, I decided to challenge the lumbering dinosaur and filed a claim against them for breaking the terms and conditions of their service contract. Although my Spanish is not good, I followed this up with a letter outlining the problem and sent it to Correos, convinced that I would hear no more.

A few days later I received a very apologetic letter from Correos, accepting full liability for the problem, and assuring me that I would receive a full refund of all postal charges. True to their word, the postman called today to give me a cash refund! Victories against these lumbering dinosaurs are few, but when they do come, the taste of victory is sweet!

Tomorrow, Tomorrow...!

I guess that many of us have a love/hate relationship with our utility companies. Somehow the electricity, water and telephone companies have little of the charisma of some of our favourite shops and suppliers that we can actually choose. In the UK, even the rigours of enforced de-nationalisation and expensive publicity and marketing campaigns seems to have done little to improve the perception of these lumbering beasts in the eyes of the general public. The same is true in Spain and the Canary Islands, where we are currently going though the same tedious processes of being offered 'alternative suppliers' for our electricity, water and telephones calls - even though we all know that it comes from exactly the same source! I was really touched to receive a letter a few days ago from the old nationalised company assuring me that they would give me a two per cent discount off our electricity bill - if we stayed with them. They omitted to mention that prices were going up far in excess of this anyway! However, I digress.

Last week, I called the electricity company to advise them of a change of postal address. Not that I am actually moving house, I am not, but a post office box tends to be a more reliable way of receiving mail rather than having it lobbed over the gate, as is the favoured method of delivery by our usual postman, the part time drag queen I mentioned in an earlier Twitter, and who clearly has his mind on other things!

As usual the telephone lines were very busy. Earlier dealings with the electricity company had always been less than successful. I was certainly prepared for a long wait with a large glass of wine and a packed lunch at the ready. The telephone rang and rang although, surprisingly, it was eventually answered by a real person, it sounded like a young woman. Over the sound of canned music, I was given a pleasant greeting and she enquired how she could help me. So far, so good. The young woman had some difficulty in making herself heard, as she shouted over the incessant loud chattering and laughter, as well as loud canned music in the background.

I made my request for a change of address and was not that surprised to hear the response, "No, it is not possible over the telephone. You must come into the office with your passport, national identity number, birth certificate," inside leg measurements and all the other requirements for pieces of paper that our bureaucratic Spanish friends seem to love so much! "Ah, so it is not possible to do this over the telephone?" I enquired. I was then told that this was not possible, but that I could send a fax to the company and this would be quite sufficient! Although I was puzzled as to how this would actually prove my identity, I had learned long ago that, apart from their love affair with paper, Spanish officials also adore fax machines - they are far more popular here than in the UK.

I was then put on hold whilst the young woman took some of the details. What was that music playing in my ear? It sounded familiar. Well, it was certainly appropriate for the electricity company, none other than a shrill song from that, in my personal opinion, ghastly, cringe-making musical, Annie (my ears are still recovering from the shock!), "Tomorrow, Tomorrow, I'll love you tomorrow, You're only a day away...!" Someone at the electricity company certainly has a sense of humour, although I doubt they are aware of the irony!

LIVING THE DREAM

Food and Drink

A Recession Busting Breakfast

In our Canarian village we are blessed with three small grocery stores. They are not very large and it can be a bit of a squash if there are more than a handful of customers in the shop at a time. Despite being surrounded by spacious, modern supermarkets in nearby large towns as well as in Las Palmas city, we have discovered, as have many villagers, that the prices in our local shops are very competitive with the larger supermarkets and usually we prefer to shop locally. There are also other benefits; for example, one shop happily delivers anything to our home, which is a boon for such items as large bottles of water and anything that is particularly heavy. They are also very reliable - items purchased are always delivered to our home later the same day and nothing seems to be too much trouble. I guess our village shops are reminiscent of village shops and post offices in the UK that have since given way to the out-of-town hypermarkets.

On one weekly shopping expedition in the village store, I patiently waited at the cheese and processed meats counter for my turn. There was an elderly Canarian woman in front of me and she seemed to be having some trouble in deciding which cheese she should buy. Eventually she stabbed her finger on the glass counter and pointed to one of large slabs, asking if she could try it. As in all the best

UK delicatessens, the shop assistant nodded and cut off a generous slice and passed it over the counter on a cardboard plate for the old woman to try. Ancient, well-worn fingers slowly crumbled the cheese into small pieces and I watched as she savoured each tiny piece of the creamy white cheese. The shop assistant, anxious to return to the girl on the till to continue the morning gossip, watched in silent anticipation.

Eventually, the old woman put the cardboard plate back on the counter with some satisfaction, looked inside the glass cabinet for a second time and pointed to another large slab of cheese of a different variety. Again, she asked for a sample. The shop assistant nodded and cut off another slice, this time not quite as large as the first, and handed it to the elderly woman. Again, she broke it into tiny pieces, savouring each delicious mouthful with relish before nodding and placing her plate on the counter. To my increasing disbelief, once again the old woman repeated the process of pointing to yet another slab of different cheese and, without a word, the shop assistant cut of a small piece and handed it over for the old woman to sample.

By now, there was a small queue of people patiently waiting their turn. Most Canarians are very tolerant by nature (this tends to distinguish them from their Peninsular Spanish counterparts) and we all stood watching with some amusement as the old woman then pointed to some slices of ham. Again, a sample of ham was handed to the old woman to try. This same process was then repeated for two different varieties of olives - each time the old woman savouring each delicious mouthful with considerable enjoyment.

Eventually the old woman appeared to be satisfied. At last she smiled and pointed once again through the glass display cabinet to the first slab of cheese that she had sampled. We all heaved a sigh of considerable relief as a small chunk was cut off, weighed, and carefully wrapped in both plastic as well as tin foil and was finally handed to the old woman, who popped it into the jacket of her cardigan and wandered over to the till to pay for her purchase.

Walking home from the shop I wondered if the old woman repeated this process regularly in all three of our village shops? Certainly, the shop assistant seemed to know the routine well and I admired her uncomplaining attempts to satisfy her customer. I wonder just how accommodating the Saturday girl would be to this old woman in a Tesco's delicatessen in the UK? "There's no such thing as a free lunch," they say, but maybe there is such a thing as a free breakfast!

Marmite soldier, anyone?

There is no doubt that many readers are in uproar after hearing about a most worrying series of thefts in the UK. If you are not already aware, a current wave of thefts from garages and small shops in Northamptonshire is terrorising the UK for fear that this moral decline spreads beyond the confines of this county.

So what is the object of this desire? Well, no other than a much-loved (and often hated) addition to a decent slice of toast - Marmite! Many reports of this heinous crime have been noted in recent weeks, but the current spate of incidents has taken the police by surprise and is particularly alarming with 18 jars of Marmite, with a 'black market' value of around £50, being taken from a single garage shop. The thefts have become so serious that shop owners are now being forced to keep this unique product under the counter for their more discerning customers, or not stocking it at all for the time being. We live in fear of an imminent Marmite shortage.

Marmite can, in my opinion, be equated with Blackpool or Benidorm - you either love it or hate it. There simply is no halfway point. Personally, I like nothing better than a slice of hot toast and butter with a thin spread of Marmite with my morning coffee. Our dog, Barney, who sadly died recently, loved it too and he would sit beside me adoringly, salivating until it was his turn for a Marmite soldier, which he gobbled down with great glee. Bella, our Spanish fruit bat-type dog, on the other hand, obviously detests the stuff and although she knows better then to decline the offer, takes the offending morsel grudgingly between her teeth, so as not to touch her mouth with the foul sticky stuff and swallows as quickly as she can before gulping down a bowlful of water. You see, you either love it or hate it.

Despite promises from the various British supermarkets that have come and gone over the years, occasional appearances in Spar or Carrefour, a regular supply does seem to be missing. European Governments would do well to remember that the temporary shortage of Marmite's main competitor in Australia - Vegemite, very nearly toppled a government!

Marmite, along with the elusive 'J' cloth, pump action Sensodyne toothpaste, Linda McCartney sausages and vegetarian gravy granules are just a few of the products that I always ask friends to bring back to the island for me whenever they visit the UK, or maybe if visiting family and friends wish to bring us something special.

Having just returned to the island from the UK, and being an avid Marmite lover, I can already imagine some unkind comments from a few people who know of my love of this product. I can assure my family, friends and readers that I have nothing to do with this incident. Besides I already have a dozen or so jars safely stored at home - just in case!

Tortillas are not always what they seem

I cannot pretend that it has always been easy being a lifelong vegetarian. From my early childhood days in my home village in fenland Lincolnshire, where my parents thought that I would expire from lack of protein, to my current life in the Canary Islands, I have had to ask, demand, compromise, challenge and examine the contents of my plate very closely. The early days in Spain were very difficult at times, and often still are in some of the more remote villages in the Canary Islands. Many locals thought vegetarians very odd, although would usually attempt to understand and provide an excellent salad or maybe a Spanish Omelette. This is often where the problems began.

Working on the principle that I will not eat anything that has had a face or a mother (and please don't get me on to the subject of eggs!) you first need to understand that many Spanish and Canarians still think of tuna as a plant. Of course tuna is not living and breathing and it is perfectly acceptable to include it as an item in a salad... Fortunately, there are now many cafe bars and restaurants in the Spain, as well as in the Canary Islands, who now know that tuna is most definitely not a plant, but a fish. Yes, but, how about some ham...

There is a small, traditional, yet very friendly bar, just outside Torrevieja, where I would often call in for a glass of wine and maybe some tortilla. It was family owned and I quickly realised that the tortillas were not of the wet and slimy pre-packaged variety that you can easily buy in the supermarket, but a delicious, genuine homemade Spanish tortilla - made by grandma herself. The barman very quickly introduced me to grandma and she beamed with toothless delight when I complimented her upon the quality of her tortillas. From that day on, whenever I called in, there would always be slices of freshly cooked tortilla available. Often the flavours would change and sometimes the old lady would add cabbage, maybe peas and sometimes carrots to the traditional mix of potato and onion, and they were always delicious.

As time went on, the experience began to remind me a little of Letitia, the weird, well meaning old lady in the TV comedy, the Vicar of Dibley, because there were amazing similarities between grandma's experiments and Letitia who, if you recall, would make amazing, yet disgusting, concoctions with fish paste, jam, anchovies and chocolate sauce - all at the same time. I could never be too sure as to what would be the ingredients of the day. I felt trouble brewing, but was never quite sure when it would strike.

Fortunately, on one memorable day, just as I was about to tuck into a slice of the latest experiment that, I was told, contained chopped red peppers, I had the uneasy feeling that all was not quite what it seemed. I removed the mouthful that I was currently chewing into a napkin and examined the contents closely. No, it was not red pepper; it was finely chopped ham. I walked over to the bar and the old lady appeared from behind the plastic strip curtain. She beamed her toothy smile and looked at my enquiring face expecting her usual compliment. This time I shook my head and she looked bitterly disappointed. In faltering Spanish I explained that the tortilla contained ham and that vegetarians do not eat meat. She looked angry, her hand swept up in horror and a babble of unintelligible Spanish flooded in my direction. Her son shook his head sadly and explained in faltering English that grandma was bitterly disappointed with me as she thought vegetarians ate ham. She could not understand why I had declined her latest tasty offering and took it as a personal insult. It was clear that I would no longer be welcome and I fled.

From that day to this I will only eat genuine Spanish Omelette - tortilla de patatas or maybe one with onion - tortilla de cebolla, containing the traditional mix of potatoes and/or onion! Whatever I am told about the innocence of the ingredients of the tortilla on offer I decline gratefully. Sorry grandma, but real vegetarians most certainly do not eat ham!

A Drop of the Hard Stuff

A couple of years ago I bought a rather good camera on eBay. It was only slightly used and I reasoned that it would serve my interest in photography for a few years to come. It was one of those, to some, unnecessarily large single lens reflex digital cameras with all the bells and whistles and megapixels that anyone could wish for.

For the last two years the camera has served me well, taking high quality photographs in readiness for my next book. As and when I could afford it, I bought an additional lens, better flash and so on.

Imagine my horror when, towards the end of August, I retrieved the camera from its resting place in a cupboard and discovered that it had partly melted. Maybe 'melted' is a bit of an exaggeration, but the rubber/plastic handgrip and side panel were now oozing a sticky black gunge - very similar to melting tarmac that we see in the UK after a particularly hot day. The black stickiness was so unpleasant that I could not hold the camera without it leaving a thick black residue on my hand. It covered my shirt in a black oily stain when it brushed against the rubber handgrip and side of the camera. Obviously, it was almost impossible to compose a decent photograph!

I know we have had a very hot August with temperatures approaching 40°C on our terrace, but I am quite sure that cameras are meant to withstand extremes of heat and cold, otherwise there would be no jungle or arctic photos to be seen anywhere!

My first port of call was, of course, the Internet, as this is the modern way to solve most problems. There are few things in life that have not happened to someone else, somewhere before. My search proved fruitless and so I posted a message on one of the camera web-forums asking for help. I received one reply suggesting that I may wish to apply Johnson's Baby Powder regularly to the offending parts of the camera. Now, I know that this stuff is great for babies' bottoms, but I also know enough about cameras to realise that applying a fine dust, however gentle on the skin, anywhere near an expensive camera is just asking for trouble.

I visited several camera shops whose sales staff looked at the camera with disgust. One suggested that I may like to buy a new one, and the other two sales assistants made that sharp sucking-in-of-breath-between-the-teeth sound that I hate so much. It always means expensive trouble. I was right, and fled on both occasions.

I sent emails to two camera repair specialists in the UK. One resisted the temptation to reply and the other suggested it might be my sweaty hands - I think not! Eventually, I received a reply from the camera manufacturer suggesting that I may like to send the camera to their service division and that the cost would be about £200 to replace the handgrip and side panel! This, I suspect, is rather more than the camera is worth.

I sat and reflected over the day's problems with my favourite tipple - a neat Scotch. I came to the conclusion that I was yet again the victim of planned obsolescence that affects so many appliances and gadgets nowadays. Suddenly, I had an idea! I grabbed the nearest piece of clean cloth to hand - my unused handkerchief - and dipped it into my glass of the wonderful golden liquid. I then rubbed the cloth gently over the rubber handgrip and, to my immense surprise and pleasure the black sticky residue began to disappear. I poured more Scotch onto the cloth and rubbed the offending pieces of rubber.

I am now pleased to report that my camera once again looks like new. The black rubber handgrip and side panels now gleam, and they are no longer sticky or leave a residue on my shirt. All it took was a very small quantity of whisky and a clean handkerchief!

Not only does my favourite tipple taste good and help me to unwind, and is a wonderful cure for colds and flu, but is now highly recommended to clean black, sticky gunge off expensive cameras. Cheers!

Environmental

Saving the Planet with a Plastic Bag

I am thoroughly confused about climate change. Like many people I am confused by what seems the overriding evidence that it is man who is responsible for climate change and that unless we act quickly and with determination our planet is doomed. On the other hand, we have the so-called sceptics who maintain that these dire predictions are the result of political and economic reasons and have nothing at all to do with man-made climate change. I guess I am now an agnostic on this issue, but surely if there is any doubt at all, it is best to be on the safe side. Best not to play Russian Roulette with our planet - we may not live to regret it!

This brings me to the thorny subject of a certain French supermarket chain of which I am not too fond. It is one of those annoying stores where I have had a number of arguments about things that annoy me, and which have met with a totally disinterested response. Witnessing and commenting about an elderly woman who tripped over a box of bananas left in one of the aisles due lack of lighting - you actually need a torch to read some of the labels on a cloudy day - met with the defensive comment, "Ah, you see, we switch lights off because we are trying to save electricity and the planet." Never mind the poor old soul being carted out of the store on a shopping trolley like a sack of potatoes and into a waiting ambulance...

On another occasion, whilst buying fruit and vegetables, something I try to avoid in this particular store as they are far cheaper and fresher in my village, I complained that several items on the shelf were already rotting and it was clear what was left would not last long once it had been taken home. It was during a calima when we all know that the island becomes unbearably hot for a few days and that, if possible, it is best to stay indoors with a cooling fan or air conditioning. On these rare occasions most food stores make the most of their air conditioning whereas this supermarket had it switched off. It was clear from watching the staff, who I noticed were already very pink at the gills and sweating uncomfortably whilst the sensible ones had their heads stuck inside freezing cabinets for relief. The lack of customers in the store should have given management a clue that maybe it was too hot to be comfortable or safe. I mentioned this point to one of their 'customer service team' who gave me the reassurance. "Ah, that is because we have the air conditioning switched off. We are trying to save electricity and the planet."

A few days ago I arrived at the checkout with a small quantity of shopping. I usually prefer to shop locally, but my needs were urgent and time was short. I paid the cashier and noticed that there were no plastic bags and asked if I could have some. The cashier shook his head with a smirk. "No, we no longer give them out. You can buy one if you like, but it will cost you 10 cents."

I shook my head and demanded to know why this sudden change of policy was introduced, whilst tempted to tell him exactly where he could place my shopping - back on the shelves where it came from, but thought better of it.

"Ah that is because we are trying to save plastic and the planet," was the immediate, and predictable, reply.

Now, I am fully aware of the evils of plastic bags and particularly the problems that they cause landfill sites and, yes, it would have been better if I had arrived at the checkout with my own bags, but I had not. What particularly annoys me is that it is not that plastic bags are no longer to be used, but that we now have to pay for them. I wonder if anyone has noticed a reduction in prices in return?

I also like consistency and I cannot see why, if the store is trying to save plastic as well as the planet, they are now giving out plastic bags freely at the entrance to the store in order to security seal purchases made at other stores in the shopping centre. At least I used to recycle the old plastic bags for dog poo!

Scotch and Oestrogen, Sir?

A few days ago I made a return visit to Firgas, a delightful small town to the north of Gran Canaria, and a municipality in its own right. This is the home of Firgas bottled water - sparkling mineral water, which originates from a plentiful spring some three miles from the town. It is said that the bottling plant produces around 200,000 bottles a day - no wonder it is popular throughout the islands.

Before moving to Spain, I was totally opposed to the idea of drinking bottled water. I felt strongly that the making and discarding of plastic bottles was not environmentally friendly and, in any case, I had read somewhere that the plastics that the bottles were made from contained many harmful substances that polluted the liquids they contained. Apparently, the environmentalists told us, we are unwittingly absorbing cancer causing chemicals from the plastic into our bodies. No doubt the same can be said for many food and drink products and not just water in plastic bottles. Anyway, I reasoned, I certainly wouldn't be paying for bottled water. After all, I had been drinking the stuff right out of the tap for all my life and it hadn't done me any harm, or had it?

One of the first things that we were told when we arrived in the Costa Blanca was "not to drink the tap water". I knew this, of course, from the many holidays that we had already spent in the country, and it was reassuring to be told by an experienced 'expat' that "tap water is quite safe to drink, but you might get a stomach upset from the minerals if you do... Drink bottled water instead". With this advice from one who knew, I cast my inhibitions aside and decided to drink bottled water instead. After all, when one moves to another country it is important to show some flexibility...! We also invested in a rather clever water filtration and chiller system. These units are supposed to purify and remove any harmful substances that may have found their way into tap water, as well as removing most of those nasty tasting chemical additives and it would mean no more plastic bottles.

Bar room gossip and chat can be a wonderful source of, mostly inaccurate, information for the newly arrived 'expat'! The influence of cheap booze and the fact that few expats take the trouble to learn Spanish before they arrive in the country can result in outrageous claims and notoriously unreliable information freely given to anyone who will listen. However, on one occasion, I had the good fortunate to meet with a, still sober, engineer who worked for one of the water companies in the UK. He confirmed that most substances in ordinary tap water could be rendered harmless by filtration, adding chemicals and the rest, with the exception of oestrogen. I pricked up my ears upon hearing this piece of information and quickly learned that too much oestrogen is certainly not too good for you. Indeed, in men, too much of the stuff can lead to the development of breasts. Now, gentlemen, unless you really crave for a nice pair of breasts, or are seriously considering a career change to become a drag queen possibly, it is best to avoid too much of the stuff. Sadly, my engineer friend gave me little more information than I have repeated here. He had already downed more than his fair share of lager before announcing that this was why he always stuck to drinking lager and rarely touched a glass of water. "But surely...?" I began, and then thought better than to discuss the subject with him any further.

If you 'Google' oestrogen (or estrogen) you will quickly discover the definition that "Oestrogen is the main sex hormone in women and is essential to the menstrual cycle." This is lovely for the ladies, I am sure, but I am not sure that we should be drinking the stuff in our 'Café con Leché'. Indeed, can you imagine placing an order at the bar for a "Double Scotch and Oestrogen"? Ah, you already have.

Returning to Firgas bottled sparkling water. It is a lovely refreshing drink and I am reassured that it is sold in glass bottles. Cheers!

The Canarian Calima

Newly arrived residents and visitors to the Canary Islands often mistake the Calima as haze or overcast weather. Actually, it is a fine layer of very oppressive dust and sand laden wind that covers the islands occasionally during the winter months, but more often during the summer. Right, now for the geography and science lesson.

The Calima, like it's 'big brother', the Sirocco, blows from an area of high pressure usually over Northern Africa and the Sahara and is driven by South Easterly winds out into the Atlantic and over the Canary Islands. Such storms and the rising warm and humid air can lift dust 5,000 metres or so above the Atlantic blanketing hundreds of thousands of square miles of the eastern Atlantic Ocean with a dense cloud of Saharan sand, often reaching as far as the Caribbean.

The Calima originates in the Saharan desert, where a unique microclimate exists, known as the Saharan Air Layer. This consists of a dry, dust-laden pocket of air that forms over the desert, normally between spring and summer. This pocket then hangs over the desert up to a height of a couple of kilometres into the atmosphere. However, if the wind swings round to blow across the Canary Islands from the south east, it can bring a Calima at any time of year. It picks up the Saharan Air Layer and drives a proportion of it across the water to the islands, whilst the rest is dispersed across the Atlantic or via rainfall.

The effects of this dust storm can be felt in a variety of ways. Most notable is the sudden rise in temperatures that a Calima brings – even in the winter months. The dust which lies in the atmosphere creates a barrier for rising hot air, trapping it closer to the earth's surface. Combine this with the fact that it is often a hot wind that brings the Calima here in the first place and it is easy to see why they result in a mini heat wave.

As can be expected when a substantial quantity of fine dust particles is suspended in the air, the Calima often causes a range of side effects for local residents' and holidaymakers' health alike. Particularly for those suffering from asthma and other related breathing difficulties. It can also irritate the sinuses, eyes, ears, throat and stomach as a result of exposure.

Canarian Calimas can last anything from a few hours to about a week. However, the Calima generally lasts for two to three days on Gran Canaria and during the summer months is accompanied by a significant rise in air temperature. The air turns a reddish-brown shade. This fine film of dust and sand can creep through doors and windows and creates havoc with outside patios, outdoor furniture and cars, which all need a good wash and scrub when it ends.

Sometimes locusts are also blown over from the Sahara region of North Africa, but they usually don't live long after their journey, which is probably just as well for the farmers and gardeners of the islands. The dust from calimas that originate in the Sahara can be carried across the Atlantic Ocean much further than the Canary Islands and can reach as far as Florida and Puerto Rico (and not the town in Gran Canaria).

Conditions can deteriorate to such an extent that it sometimes forces public life and transport to a standstill. In January 2002, the airport at Santa Cruz in Tenerife had to be closed because of poor visibility - pilots could see for less than 50 metres in front of their planes.

Locals tell me that the best thing to do is, and my apologies for this very sexist statement, if you are a man, to stay indoors with a few mates and a ready supply of cans of beer and watch football on the television, whilst the women usually head for the local commercial centres!

The Magic Blue Ball

It was just one of those regular shopping trips to the local hypermarket. Not only do I like the store but, as a lover of all gadgets, the self service checkout machines do intrigue me, despite the fact that I invariably have to seek assistance from the patient lady supervising the operation. After all, when is a tomato not a tomato? When it is Canarian and on special offer is the answer. How about multiple items? Hmm, well practice does make perfect they say.

"Have you tried one of those new Magic Wash Balls?" asked our friend, who was lingering by the checkouts. "They're wonderful. They're hard to get, you know, but they have just got some in today. George swears by them."

I was intrigued. Anything that George swore by was well worth checking out. However, intrigue was replaced by cynicism when I heard that this magic blue ball, now apparently all the rage in Portugal and Spain, did away with the need to use washing powders, liquids or indeed any of the less than environmentally attractive yet expensive additives that we have all been conditioned to use over the years. It seemed that one Magic Ball lasted for at least 1000 washes (around 3 years), did not need topping up with any expensive refills and, as well as being environmentally friendly, meant that a low temperature wash could be used.

"It can't be. How does it work?" I asked.

"We don't really know, but we are hoping to pick up a couple now. As I said, George swears by them."

As I handed over 15 euros to the cashier for this very doubtful piece of plastic I could hear my mother extolling the virtues of Persil, Omo and Daz in my ears. All these distant memories from childhood were now to be replaced by one rather uninspiring blue ball.

Two months on I am pleased to announce to the world that it does work! I have since bought a second Magic Blue Ball, as advised by the manufacturers for use with a very large wash. I calculate that we have already saved a small fortune in washing liquids and powders, not to mention reduced electricity and water bills. No longer is the nasty powder clogging up the pipes and drains, or polluting seas and rivers that, I have to confess, does make me feel a little smug.

"What about the perfume?" asked one cynic, her eyes flashing dangerously at the mere suggestion that she should abandon her Persil whiteness (and it shows! You see, how the advertising jingles have got to me?). I gently reminded her that we wash to make clothes clean and not just for the nice smell. In any case, I suggested, she could always use fabric conditioner for the perfume. My reasoning fell on deaf ears.

Yes, I am now an unashamed apostle for the Magic Ball. I tell everyone how wonderful it is, but I have learned not to mention it to those who, shall we say, are a little set in their ways. After all, not everyone wants to save money and are happy to clog their machines and pollute the environment.

The Week The Planes Stopped Flying

The day has been silent. We live quite close to the airport and are used to seeing the many flights arriving each day with their cargos of white, pallid, passengers, released from the tight grip of a Northern European winter, looking forward to the comforting warmth of the Canarian sun. Often, we see the same passengers a week later at the airport, this time in the departures queues, looking browner and healthier, if not sadder, as they prepare for their weary flights home.

Today was different. There were no queues of frustrated travellers and irritating tour representatives herding their reluctant passengers into long queues to await their turns at the check-in desks. The waiting area was empty. The glaring departures board screamed the one word that no one wanted to read, 'CANCELLED'.

The volcanic ash from Iceland has done its worst for our islands, already teetering from the effects of recession. Hoteliers, bar and restaurant owners and shopkeepers, all looking forward to the heady days of a springtime tourist revival, shook their heads as they shared and commiserated together the events of one of the worst weeks in the tourist business on the islands. The planes had stopped coming and in their hand-to-mouth business, so too had the hard earned currency that would help them to keep their businesses open for another season.

Back in the airport, I spotted activity around the customer service desk of one of the low cost airlines.

"I need to get home before then, my son's medication has run out," cried the grey haired mother with her disabled son standing silently at her side.

"We'll give you a flight back next week, but other than that you are on your own," came the harsh reply to one desperate family, surrounded by pushchairs, a crying baby and a screaming toddler.

"You pay nothing and you get f**k all," came the words of an angry young man clutching a rucksack. "I should have known. I will never fly with this bunch of cowboys again."

The customers of another low cost airline - the one with the smart orange tracksuits - fared rather better. This airline appeared to be treating their customers with the respect that they deserved. Not only were they booking passengers into alternative flights, but they were also putting them up in hotels. They may not have been where they wanted to be, but at least their clients would not have to spend a night on the beach.

The local television crew arrived to film the antics and the anger outside the office of the low cost airline. The passengers instinctively turned their backs against their cameras - after all, why should their misery be the stuff of the evening's television entertainment?

I left the airport, disturbed and saddened and began to muse upon a world without the precious, noisy, fuel-guzzling machines that dominate our planet. Our reliance upon these monsters of the sky, carrying their bellyfuls of passengers to exotic destinations is something that we all take for granted. Once they stop flying, even for a few days, holidays and finances are ruined, perishable goods such as fresh fruit, vegetables, food items and flowers lay rotting in warehouses in Las Palmas, London and Nairobi and national economies begin to crumble.

Maybe one day in the future the planes really will stop flying. Children will gather to hear tales of giant flying metal birds carrying people to destinations in the sun. Will we also be telling them of tales of complaining passengers, sitting in silence watching noisy cartoons on large screens, who have only paid the price of the latest best seller for a ticket to a far away destination? Will we tell them about the food and drink in plastic trays and beakers and the complaints that it is not as good as they could get in their local takeaways? What about the planes themselves? Will we visit them in museums and both admire and loathe them for the way in which they changed our planet forever?

In a week of chaos and inconvenience, maybe we should be grateful for the silence, and the opportunity that the volcanic ash from Iceland has given us to reflect upon a world without these whales of the sky, and begin to imagine a flight-free world in their place?

Water from Wind

Turning water into wine is a great idea, but how about turning wind into water? I have always loved windmills. Their graceful form and natural motion have always fascinated me. However, I know that many people also hate the sight of them as yet another of man's intrusion upon a beautiful landscape. However, now that a new era of limited fuel supplies is upon us, harnessing the wind to provide a cheap and sustainable source of fuel to feed our unending desire for electricity seems much more attractive.

A drive to a Canarian village near my home, Pozo Izquierdo, near Vecindario, will provide a physics lesson that is not easily forgotten. Not only is it a great place for a good walk with the dog and some fresh air, but you will be in the centre of a wind farm that not only produces electricity from the wind, but also any excess electricity produced is used to desalinate water from the seawater that surrounds this island paradise.

Saving water, one of the island's scarcest resources due to the lack of rain, has led to extensive research in the desalination of seawater and using wind power to operate small desalination plants. The islands are not short of wind power – the Trade Winds, with their moderate speed and direction, are constant throughout the year. This technology and ideas have since been exported to many other parts of the world.

One of the main objections to wind farms has always been that they produce a varying amount of electricity. This variability of supply in the electricity grid means that there must be other power generators, such as gas fired units, that can come 'on line' at short notice – in order to avoid wide fluctuations of power and your television or washing machine blowing up. Keeping these generators 'at the ready' is an expensive use of resources and is often the quoted reason for not using wind powered generators.

Now this is the clever part. The desalination of water is an expensive process and requires a lot of electricity. However, scientists found that the wind generation of electricity and the process of desalination of water can work together successfully for the simple reason that electricity cannot be cheaply stored, but water can. Using surplus electricity from wind farms such as the one in Pozo Izquierdo to desalinate seawater is the ideal solution. When there is a falling amount of surplus electricity, the number of desalination units operating is reduced. The water produced when the wind farms are in full production can then be stored relatively cheaply until required. Clever stuff, eh?

Cars from Bananas

I like eating bananas and, since coming to live in Gran Canaria, I am now a passionate advocate for this humble fruit, which, incidentally, is also called "the fruit of the wise". From a health point of view, it really is a wonderful addition to the weekly shopping list, as it contains vitamins and minerals essential for the human body. Bananas contain Vitamin C, potassium and dietary fibre, but do not contain sodium, fat or cholesterol. Bananas also contain three natural sugars, sucrose, fructose and glucose and gives an instant and substantial boost of energy. They also contain Vitamin B6, which helps protect the immune system and the functioning of the central nervous system. Pretty good stuff, eh?

Yes, I like bananas. Not those perfectly shaped and tasteless Caribbean Eurobanana varieties that grace the shelves of the UK supermarkets, but that gem of all bananas - the Canarian banana. Small and sometimes misshapen they may be, but the creamy yellow flesh and sweet taste make them very special.

Maybe I am just a little biased, because after all, I am surrounded by them. However, 18% of all the bananas eaten in Europe are produced in the Canary Islands, and very important to the islands' economy they are too. Amazingly, around 10 million banana plants are grown in Gran Canaria each year - that is a lot of bananas for one small island, and this produces an awful lot of waste.

In the past, banana plant waste was used as a support for growing the equally popular tomato plants, and in crafts such as basket making and artificial flowers. The plant waste was also used as fodder for cattle and goats, but factory farming has replaced this with concentrated feeds. Today, this vegetable waste is deposited in ravines on the islands where they naturally decompose. An estimated 25,000 tonnes each year of natural fibre is found in this waste. Indeed, what a waste!

Not any more, it seems. The European Union is currently funding something called the 'Badana Project'. This imaginative scheme is focused upon developing a process that will convert this natural organic waste into plastics that will be suitable for making cars, washing machines and kayaks, to name just a few of the intended uses.

It appears that there is money in banana waste too. Judging from the list of organisations sponsoring the project with the European Union, along with universities in the Canary Islands, Spain and Belfast, and companies from the Canary Islands, Spain, the Netherlands, Hungary, Bulgaria and the UK. The old truism, "Where there's muck there's money", springs to mind. Maybe it should now read, "Where there's bananas there's plastic."

Just a few more facts about the humble banana. The word banana is derived from the Arab word "banan," which means finger and, unlike most other fruits that grow on trees, bananas grow on plants.

Incidentally, the word 'badana' from the 'Badana Project' really is the fibre obtained from layers of the banana stem and not just 'banana' spluttered by a European Union official with a bad head cold!

Seaside Burps

"Oh, I do like to be beside the seaside!" goes the familiar music hall song and maybe most of us agree with the sentiment. It is also a pretty safe bet that if you are reading this 'Twitter' you are either living by the sea or thinking about doing it!

We Brits love our traditional seaside holiday resorts. Strolling along the promenade wearing a thick pullover, gloves and scarf on a cold, wet day, breathing in the fresh sea air just makes us feel so glad to be alive, doesn't it? Alright, we also look forward to going back home to a cosy fire and a hot cup of coffee to thaw out. We Brits are mostly a hardy lot and somehow, at the time, the cold and damp didn't seem to matter too much because we were breathing in all that fresh ozone. It is just so good for us, or is it?

As a child growing up in rural Lincolnshire, it became a family tradition that if we were recovering from a cold or flu, my father would take us to Skegness for the day. "This'll blow away those germs, lad," he would say, although privately I suspected that when I got home, I would end up with pneumonia anyway. Yes, Skegness was just so bracing and that sea air, well...!

So, Skegness it was to be for much of my early life, later to be superseded by the delights of seaside resorts that I still know and love. Blackpool, Weymouth, Bournemouth, Brighton, Benidorm ...!

Benidorm, now where did that come from? Like many of us, I quickly learned that to enjoy more of the delights of the seaside that didn't require the protection of a raincoat, scarf and gloves would mean a move overseas.

As I grew older, the longing for the seaside was never far away. Those bracing walks with the dogs were quickly followed by a leisurely look through the holiday brochures to plan our next holiday in the sun. One thing was for certain, even though I didn't like the cold, wet, grey Bank Holidays by the sea in the UK, I did feel a longing to be beside a sea that was blue, clean and sparkling. Like so many before me, I dreamt of sunbathing on golden beaches, and not the muddy flats of coastal Lincolnshire.

Maybe it would be the Costa Blanca, the Costa del Sol, the Canary Islands, Portugal or further afield if funds permitted? Very quickly the dream of living by a seaside that I could visit anytime that I wished became too much, and this is why I am now living only a very short distance from the sea in the Canary Islands; a move that I am very thankful for.

So what is it that gives the seaside its distinctive flavour? The sand? The endless rolling waves or the distinctive smell maybe? Maybe it really was the "bracing ozone" that my father was convinced would do us the power of good during our period of recuperation? It took me some years to discover the truth.

So what is it that gives the sea its distinctive smell; the unmistakable whiff that we associate with summer holidays? Without wishing to ruin the romantic view of the sea that many of us share, that wonderful smell of the sea is actually due to nothing more exotic than flatulence; wind, burps and farts to you and I! Cows do it. Horses do it. People do it after drinking lager, or while eating a spicy curry. We all pass gas and lots of it too.

The seaside's familiar "bracing" smell is caused by a chemical produced by coastal bacteria, which is present in very low concentrations. Basically it is micro organisms in the sea, tucking into tasty morsels of plankton that they like best, and relieving themselves with a little burp afterwards.

So, the next time that you are enjoying a spot of sea air, just remember and be thankful for the countless millions of microscopic organisms enjoying their lunch in the sea, and relieving themselves of excess wind afterwards. Breathe deeply now!

Language and Culture

Fax Machines and Bureaucrats

Expats living in Spain will quickly become aware of how much Spanish officials adore reams of paper and boxes of rubber stamps. Well, closely, allied to this obsession is the heady adoration of that once wonderful, but now antiquated technology of the past - the fax machine. Yes, I have to admit that I used to be fascinated by the thought that a piece of paper could be put into one of these machines in London and yet, almost in real time, it would pop out from another very similar machine in New York. If you think about it, it really is a very clever process.

However, times have moved on and we now have the Internet, emails and text messages, and somehow the humble fax machine looks like something rapidly destined for a museum of 1970's technology - or is it?

Since moving to Spain I have come to realise that it is essential to have a fax machine at home or at least to have ready access to one. Its use is still demanded by the many faceless officials oiling the wheels of the Spanish bureaucratic machine. Without it, the newly arrived expat will undoubtedly face a life of complete misery and degradation. "What, you don't have a fax machine?" I can hear the bureaucrats spluttering, as they tuck into their mid-morning breakfast at their desks, a ham filled bocadillo in one hand and mobile phone in the other.

A few days ago I decided to change the bank that I use to pay one of my direct debits. My initial thoughts of a quick phone call to the company concerned to change the bank details proved not to be the case. Several hours later I am still trying to achieve what would be, in the UK, a very simple procedure. My initial telephone call earlier this morning was greeted with astonishment that I should even want to consider the process of changing a bank, followed by a request that I make another request, this time by fax, confirming what I wanted to do and giving the necessary account details. Surely I could send an email? No, it had to be a fax, Maria, the lady at the end of the phone insisted politely.

My hastily typed and faxed letter was then followed up by a return phone call from Maria. Did I really want to change the bank details? Yes, I confirmed. Well, in that case, would I send a send a letter or a document from the new bank confirming my account details? This, of course, had to be sent to Maria by fax.

Once again, I plugged in the fax machine, and this time sent another letter, together with a letter from the new bank confirming the account details. This was followed by another phone call from Maria, who was now sounding a little more aggressive, complaining that although she had received my letter and the letter from the bank - the faxed letter had omitted to include my full name and fiscal number. Would I send them another letter, preferably the front page of my cheque book, which would include both my name and account details - once again, by fax. Oh, and by the way, could I fax them a copy of my passport and residencia certificate at the same time?

Three hours later, and as I type this, a simple process that should have been dealt with in a few minutes, is still grinding on. Once again, Spanish bureaucracy is beginning to wear me down and Maria will be spending all her day changing my one direct debit and I won't get any writing done. Maybe I won't change banks after all!

Love thy neighbour - Canaries style!

There is an old saying that we get the neighbours that we deserve. I have had some lovely neighbours over the years, but there have been a few strange ones, which have left me wondering what I have done to deserve them!

Do we ever really know our neighbours? From a quick glance at the rotary clothes dryer, we know that the lady of the house next door has a liking for daring red underwear, and that the gentleman of the house likes to use his power drill early on a Sunday morning. Goodness only knows what he is doing, but surely there are only so many holes that can be drilled in a lifetime with a Black and Decker? We also know from the ghastly smell that wafts over from the adjoining wall, that barbecued fish is a speciality and a delight to look forward to each Saturday evening, whilst Wednesday afternoons is the time when mother-in-law arrives to give the house a good clean.

If we are truly honest with ourselves many of us may admit that most of us rely on our neighbours for entertainment, as well as friendship and the occasional 'cup of sugar'. Over the years, I have witnessed plots and scenarios that would put Eastenders and Coronation Street to shame. I vividly remember the dear old couple next door when we were living in the UK. Mary was a charming woman, a member of the local Women's Institute and pillar of the community and a keen ballroom dancer, who would regularly make us delicious cakes and biscuits, and occasionally walk the dogs. Little did we know at the time that she was planning to do away with her husband and run away with a bookmaker boyfriend, also a keen ballroom dancer, to Corfu on the proceeds. As she was escorted from the house into a waiting police car, we realised then that Mary's famous chocolate cake would no longer be appearing on our doorstep. It was a supremely sad day for us all. Ballroom dancing has a lot to answer for.

Even though those "very nice people next door" or "the charming couple across the street" seem respectable enough people who happily water our pot plants for us or look after the cat when we are away, or do some shopping for us if we are sick, do we really know what goes on behind those shutters? It seems not.

A recent local news item caught my eye the other day. Apparently two men living in a neighbouring town owned very similar cars - both white Ford Fiestas. One was slightly smarter and more importantly, a newer model, than the other and so one neighbour decided to switch the number plates from his own Fiesta for those from his neighbour's car. The renegade neighbour then duly parked the car as his own in the same street.

Not surprisingly, the owner of the older vehicle noticed that something was wrong and alerted the local police and told them that there was a car, identical to his own, parked in his own street. The police investigated further and noticed some cosmetic changes made to the vehicle, including new painting on the wing mirrors, a set of new hubcaps, and a new tinted rear window. The true identity of the vehicle was confirmed once the police had checked the chassis number. The police are now searching for the errant neighbour, which shouldn't take too long as these islands are quite small.

I doubt the two men will be good neighbours for some time to come, which only goes to prove that to remain good neighbours, "Thou shalt not covet thy neighbour's Fiesta"!

The Sunday Slowdown

As a child and teenager growing up in rural Lincolnshire, I always hated Sundays. For me it meant a day when nothing ever happened. I was forbidden from playing with my friends, riding my bike, playing loud music and doing the normal stuff of everyday life. Usually, I was told to "sit quietly and read a book" with maybe the highlight of being sent to Sunday school in the afternoon.

Maybe it was my grandfather's influence upon the family. He didn't believe in modern day technology. The telephone, radio and certainly not the television were considered to be loathsome instruments that were the work of the devil and steadfastly refused to have anything to do with any of them. He was a firm advocate of "The Sabbath is the Lord's Day and to hell with the rest of the world" syndrome and even shaved late on Saturday evenings so that he didn't have to lift a finger and offend the Lord on Sunday morning. I could never work out the logic of this one because surely hair grew at the same pace, even on the Sabbath?

Sunday School was another disturbing influence in my life. There are only so many of those wretched sticker stamps of religious figures that a growing lad can stick in an album without having a breakdown, assisted by the monotonous drone of a half-witted, rapidly balding Sunday School teacher. Even then I knew it was a con, because Jesus always appeared as a white-skinned tall figure with long flowing blonde hair. I knew a little geography, thanks to all those books I had to look at on Sundays, and reasoned that he couldn't have that colour skin given where he came from. Fortunately, Scott, one of my best friends, alerted me to the fact that the local sweetshop was open on Sunday afternoons and for many months after this glorious discovery we would meet there, spend the Sunday School collection money on gobstoppers, liquorice, sherbet dips and all manner of sweet junk, stuff ourselves silly and then go home claiming to have been at Sunday School all afternoon.

Later, when I went to college, the freedom of doing what I wanted, when I wanted without feeling guilty on this dreaded day was bliss and it took some getting used to. However, for me, there was still one problem. All the shops and anywhere of interest were closed on a day when I had the time to look and enjoy all that was on offer. Why did the government insist that everything was closed on Sundays? It just didn't make any sense.

Later, of course, politicians of all persuasions came to their senses and grudgingly allowed Sunday shopping, albeit within a number artificial constraints. This period of relative freedom was, initially, bliss. I could visit Tesco, B&Q and all manner of stores when I wanted. I had my own home by then and it was perfect for buying the bits and pieces needed to renovate the cottage that we were living in at the time. No, my parents, and certainly my grandfather, would not have approved of my use of a Black and Decker drill late on Sunday mornings.

Moving to Spain and the Canary Islands was a shock to the system in many ways, and certainly the Spanish attitude to Sundays. All the shops, other than those designated for tourists, are closed. The large department stores and commercial centres are closed too. There are few flights to and from the usually busy airport. There are few cars and very few people around until at least midday. It is only at about 2.00pm that I catch a sniff of the gut-wrenching, foul smelling odour of fish being barbecued by the neighbours as the family arrive for Sunday lunch.

Even the usually vociferous dogs seem to know it is a day of rest and cease their barking until at least midday. There are no children to be seen, or heard. Strangely enough, I seem to have come full circle. Maybe it is best if I settle down quietly and read my book after all.

'The Big Sleep'

Have you noticed that often when we go into a shop in the UK, and the item that we need is out of stock, we are told that it will be "in on Tuesday"? Similarly, in Spain, the response is usually the predictable, "mañana". However, this is not the case in the Canary Islands. Here we have the more elaborate response, given with a shrug of the shoulders, of "It will be about six weeks, as it has to come by boat from Barcelona". It is something, that after the initial frustrations, we learn to accept. After all, we do have the most wonderful climate and the worry about getting a certain design of wall tile quickly fades into insignificance.

Does 15 August mean anything to you? Well, it is the Feast of the Assumption, Independence Day for India, Liberation Day for South Korea and Madonna's birthday for starters. Yes, the 15 August is an important day for many people around the world and, most importantly for the good people of these small islands, it is the official beginning of 'The Big Sleep'.

I say it is the official beginning of 'The Big Sleep' because, in reality, it has really been going on since the beginning of July and will, no doubt, continue to the end of September. The 15 August is more like the 'official climax' to a summer of doing very little or maybe doing nothing at all, which is even more poignant during this period of recession and major unemployment on the islands.

As much as I enjoy living and working in Spain in general, and the Canary Islands in particular, I have to confess that I do find 15 August irritating. Of course, it is the traditional beginning of the two-week summer break taken by many people of the Mediterranean countries. After all, the days are hot and sticky and the temperature is not conducive to any form of excessive physical activity. It makes a great deal of economic, health and common sense to close down building operations and any form of manufacturing during these heady summer days, and I have no problem with this at all.

What I do have a problem with are post offices, banks and council offices. Why is it that post offices, banks and government offices also decide to reduce their opening hours at a time when the holiday season and the numbers of visitors are at their peak? Why, in the comfort of their air-conditioned palaces, do post office, bank and government staff suddenly decide to operate a go-slow for most of July, August and September?

Postal deliveries are all but suspended, customers wishing to post a postcard home or pay their water bills join an endless queue - little realising that it will be at least two hours before they escape their torment. Good natured, but wily Canarians know all about such trials of life. After all, they usually have the good sense to bring a packed lunch with them and camp inside the Post Office or bank for much of the morning and treat it is a social occasion. After all, they have been through it all so many times before!

There seems to be no concept of staggering holidays for workers in these offices, let alone providing relief staff to cover holiday absences. These services tend to grind to a near standstill, yet it only seems to be the British, Germans and Scandinavians who show any form of irritation. Most Canarians simply shrug off the inconvenience with a smile and return in September.

So, on the basis of, "If you can't beat 'em, join 'em," maybe it is time for us all to shift into another gear. Well, I'm off for a swim, a lounge on the sunbed with a good book and another gin and tonic. Have a wonderful 15 August and enjoy 'The Big Sleep'!

The End of The Siesta?

A recent report by a Spanish Government backed commission urging the country to switch its clocks to Greenwich Mean Time will, no doubt, strike at the very heart of Spanish culture and tradition, if not the Spanish psyche. The proposal is aimed at shaking up the typical Spanish daily existence – with its lengthy coffee breaks, two-hour lunches and late evening meals and is the result of a survey conducted at Spanish embassies in other European countries into host nations' daily timekeeping.

It has taken me several years to adjust to the idea of the siesta and, I have to confess, it has been one of the most difficult adjustments that I, as a Brit, have had to make in Spain. However, the initial irritation of finding that shops, offices and the like have all closed at the time when I need them most has all but disappeared, as I too have adjusted and now take part in the siesta tradition.

The siesta is a very sensible idea in a hot climate when the temperature is at its fiercest. What better than a snooze after a leisurely lunch? The siesta was born not just out of the necessity of slowing down in the afternoon heat, but the fact that, traditionally, many Spanish men and women have two, relatively low paid part-time jobs, with the second job beginning after the siesta. Typically, the Spanish working day begins at about 8.00am, with a 30-minute break at 11.00am, then lunch usually starts at 2.00pm or 3.00pm, with people returning to work about two hours later, then often working on to 8.00pm, dinner as late as 10.00pm or 11.00pm. It is a long day and the siesta has become an essential way of life for many Spanish working in towns and villages, although much less so now in the cities than in the past. However, returning to the recent report, Spain has been identified as one of the least-productive countries in Europe despite the fact that, in theory, it is the European country where most hours are spent at work.

In the Canary Islands we already have Greenwich Mean Time and the pattern of life is very similar to that on the Peninsular, so I doubt that a change to GMT would make much difference to the local way of life there either. I well recall visiting our newly built property in Gran Canaria early one afternoon to take some measurements before completion. Although the property was unlocked I could see no one working there. Initially alarmed by the lack of security, I entered the property and went upstairs only to find four workmen fast asleep on flattened cardboard boxes in the main bedroom. It was siesta time and I didn't have the heart to disturb them.

Reports such as this latest one from the strangely named, 'National Commission for the Rationalisation of Timetables' come and go and, if I am not greatly mistaken, it will take much more than a report to wrench the beloved siesta from the hearts of our newly adopted countrymen. Forgive me, I must go now, it is time for my siesta.

The Spanish Mistress and The Gym Master

I am often asked what I consider to be the essentials when planning a new life in another country. My answer is always the same, to learn the language.

I won't pretend that learning Spanish has been easy for me. It hasn't. Indeed, you could say that I am not a natural at learning languages. As an eleven-year-old I was forced to learn French, a language that I did not like. Maybe it was the teacher, the quality of teaching or simply the sound of the language that I disliked, but I quickly learned, in the style of Del Boy, that 'un petit pois' was not for me.

Latin hit me in a slightly different way. Dead and dusty it may have been, but the subject was taught in a more effective fashion and with a degree of humour by my old headmaster. He was a strict disciplinarian whom I liked and respected, and I made adequate progress. However, I could see little point in the endless conjugation and chanting of those wretched verbs: "amo, amas, amant..." that will forever ring in my ears.

Eventually, crunch time. I had already dropped Latin and was doing my best to avoid French, using a variety of avoidance tactics of which I was a master. As I completed my fifth year at the school, I was told in no uncertain terms that I had either to take on another language or it was an additional two lessons a week on the playing field. To me this possibility of yet more 'hell on earth' really was sufficient motivation to find another language very quickly.

German was an option and eagerly followed by many of my peers as we entered the sixth form. However, for me the language is far too guttural and makes sounds that I wouldn't wish to make in polite company. Now, what about Italian? Yes, a musical language that is one of beauty, sincerity and where, I was assured, my Latin would come in useful, and they really are such attractive people, aren't they? The only problem was that my school didn't offer it.

The truth finally dawned. I reasoned that I would need just three languages to do anything anywhere in the world - English, Chinese and Spanish. My request for Chinese lessons was greeted with a stony faced, disinterested stare from my housemaster before I was bawled out of his study for wasting his time. Undaunted, I decided to have a chat with one of the school secretaries, a charming young women who rather liked me. A hurried whisper when her colleague disappeared into the stock room revealed that "Spanish lessons are off for the time being". This, I learned, followed an unfortunate incident between the newly appointed young Spanish mistress and the middle-aged gym master in the sports equipment cupboard the previous week. In those days, I was far too naive and polite to ask for further details, but I had a vivid imagination. So Russian it had to be.

Sadly, that was to be a disaster too. Mr Edwards had recently returned from studying a crash course in Russian at Leningrad University and was only a few pages ahead of his students in the textbook. However, I did learn sufficient to ask about the weather in Moscow and to say "I love you" in Russian, which was a bonus.

Many years later, as a school inspector in Wales, I was amazed at the ease with which four- and five-year-old English-speaking children could learn a second language - Welsh. My exposure to these children in the playground during break times, experiencing the ease with which they switched from their mother tongue to another, admittedly very difficult language to learn, both humbled and amazed me.

Learning Spanish later in life is not easy. However, I am pleased to say that I can now understand far more of what is said and written and I have growing confidence in being able to speak the language. That young Spanish teacher and the gym master in the sports cupboard at my old school have a lot to answer for, don't you think?

Not exactly cool...!

Who remembers the Reliant Robin? If you are of a certain age, you will remember the Reliant three-wheeler - the much loved (and tolerated) ageing, battered transport of Del Boy and Rodney of TV's 'Only Fools and Horses' fame. Apart from having only three wheels to worry about, this remnant of British motoring history's main claim to notoriety was that it could be driven on just a provisional or motorcycle licence; it did not require the full driving test.

I remember only too well the fleeting temptation of getting such a vehicle shortly after obtaining my first provisional licence, but as a student I could afford neither motorcycle nor three-wheeler at the time anyway, and so the idea was quickly forgotten.

This brief recollection of the past brings me to the situation regarding the little Aixim cars that are so often seen tootling along the roads between Las Palmas and Maspalomas in Gran Canaria (and, I guess, much of Spain, France, Italy and Portugal). These irritating little cars are usually very easy to spot, as they rarely move faster than 30 mph and are often trailing behind on the verges of many roads, leading a parade of angry drivers with faster vehicles frantically tooting their horns.

These vehicles can be described as 'micro-cars' and the main reason for buying them appears to be that they can be driven without any licence at all over here. This seems to be an anomaly in the motoring laws and I understand that the police are anxious to review the qualifications for driving them - for obvious reasons! I don't think I have ever seen one in the UK, probably because they are classified as a quad bike, in view of their weight and power output. This, very sensibly requires either a full driving licence or a full, unlimited capacity motorcycle licence to legally drive them in the UK. However, this may change in the future, as these little cars are very economical to run with a relatively spacious body made from a strong alloy frame, covered with non-rust plastic panels. Their low-emission engines (which sound a little like motor mowers 'on heat') make them exceptionally 'green' vehicles; and it is now possible to get various versions that run on electricity. No doubt we shall be seeing many more of these 'kerb crawlers' in the future!

Historical

Greenwich Mean Time and the Canary Islands

Maybe the real reason why time traveller, Doctor Who, has a continuing pre-occupation with sorting out problems with aliens in the City of London is not really to do with ever shrinking location budgets at the BBC, but more to do with the fact that Greenwich is the centre of time. A recent news item celebrating the 125th anniversary of the decision to make the Greenwich Meridian the centre of time, reminded me of a history lesson that I still remember from my school days. Co-incidentally, it also has an interesting link with the Canary Islands. Maybe this was the true beginning of my journey to these wonderful islands.

The Greenwich Meridian is an imaginary and arbitrary line that cuts through Spain, UK, France, Algeria and Ghana. It divides the Earth into east and west in much the same way as the Equator divides it into north and south. It enables us to navigate the globe, as well as synchronising the world's clocks. However, this has not always been the case.

Before the all-important decision 125 years ago to make Greenwich the centre of world time, many countries and, indeed, large towns kept their own local time. This was based upon the hours of daylight and there were no international rules as to when the day would start or finish. With the growth of railways crossing international borders and marine activity, it became essential to set a global time. Before an important meeting in Washington took place in 1884 there were, in Europe alone, some 20 different meridians - you can imagine the confusion!

The Washington meeting, naturally, brought with it many different views, no doubt based upon national self-interest. The final conclusion was to make Greenwich the standard for setting time with a vote of 22 to one, with only San Domingo voting against and Brazil and, predictably, France, abstaining. France suggested that the new agreed meridian should run through the Canary Islands, and this suggestion was not just French awkwardness - it had some foundation.

Back in AD 127, the Greek astronomer, Ptolemy, made astronomical observations from Alexandria in Egypt. Ptolemy selected the Fortunate Islands (the Canaries) as the physical location of the prime meridian when he created an accurate grid system upon which the location of individual cities from the farthest known land west to the farthest known land east could be accurately placed. From that time onwards, early Mediterranean navigators used the meridian through the Canaries, as their first, or prime, meridian as they were then thought to be the most western part of the habitable globe. During the 15th and 16th centuries, when the peoples of Western Europe emerged as sea traders, almost every maritime nation used as a prime meridian, a meridian passing through its own territory. The

French, for example, used the meridian of Paris; the Dutch, that through Amsterdam; and the English the meridian through London. You can only imagine the chaos and confusion and inconvenience caused to mariners by the existence of a multitude of prime meridians!

So you see the Canary Islands have a strong place in history in setting the centre of world time. Imagine the prestige (and confusion) if the world's clocks were set to Canaries Mañana Time and not Greenwich Mean Time!

World War Heroes

One of the many things that I love about our island in the sun is the 'live and let live' approach of its people. No, I don't mean the thousands of tourists, but the true Canarian people, those who were born and have stayed in this little corner of Paradise. As long as it is broadly legal and does not interfere with anyone else, in the main, anything goes. For many of its present day expat population, with its heady mix of faith, culture, colour and sexuality, it takes time to get used to not being judged. Maybe this stems from the time, it is said, when Spain's General Franco, intolerant of gay men in the military, would ship them off to Gran Canaria, which became a kind of penal colony for homosexuals. Whether there is real historical substance to this claim or whether it is an urban myth, I do not know for sure, but it sounds reasonable enough to me!

For me, one of the real unsung heroes of the Second World War was the code-breaker, Alan Turing. It was thanks to this mathematical genius that the war against Nazi Germany ended when it did. He managed to intercept and crack ingenious coded messages that gave detailed information to the Allies about the activities of German U-boats. However, there was only one problem with Alan Turing - he was gay.

Alan's reward for his pivotal role in cracking intercepted messages was quickly forgotten when, in 1952, he was prosecuted for 'indecency' after admitting a sexual relationship with a man. As an 'alternative' to imprisonment, this unsung war hero was given 'chemical castration' - a newly devised treatment for such 'disorders' at the time. In 1954, at the age of 41, he killed himself by eating a poisoned apple. I rather like this part of the tragedy - the ending is just so dramatic!

Or was this the end of Alan Turing? This amazing man is also credited with creating the beginnings of computer technology and artificial intelligence, which led to the development of one of the first recognisable modern computers. Alan Turing's brilliance and personal life came to the attention of present day computer programmer, Dr. John Graham-Cumming, who began a petition asking for a posthumous apology from the government. Many thousands of people signed it and the previous UK Prime Minister, Gordon Brown, finally apologised for how Alan Turing was treated in the 1950s. Whether it was through political motivation or genuine compassion for this brilliant man, and I like to think it is the latter, he said that "on behalf of the British government, and all those who live freely thanks to Alan's work, I am very proud to say: we're sorry, you deserved so much better."

My thoughts also go out to the many thousands of gay men and woman who have been persecuted over the years - just for being themselves.

All this serious stuff brings me back home to Gran Canaria. Spain's General Franco certainly had his faults, but I cannot help thinking that being shipped off to a life in the sun in the penal colony of Gran Canaria, just for being gay, was a far preferable alternative to 'chemical castration'!

The Virgin and the Pines

Tuesday 8 September is a very important day in Gran Canaria and one that is ignored at your peril! Not only is it yet another essential public holiday, complete with a very convenient bridging day on the day before and, no doubt, the day after - if not the rest of the week, but it is also a fiesta day when homage is paid to the Virgin of the Pines - the Patron Saint of Gran Canaria. Whatever your religious affiliation or beliefs, it can only mean one thing on this island - party, party, party!

The town of Teror is one of the most attractive towns in Gran Canaria, and is the site for this most important of religious festivals. Visiting Teror during the week of the festival is highly recommended, with one important caveat that I will mention later, as this pretty town is decked out in all its splendour and ready to receive thousands of visitors for this annual festival and pilgrimage.

Legend has it that in 1481 a vision of the Virgin Mary appeared to some shepherds on the top of a pine tree, and since then the Virgin of the Pines has played an important role in the history and the everyday life of the people of Gran Canaria. Pope Pius XII proclaimed her patron saint of the island in 1914 and Teror, with its beautiful church, became the religious capital of the island. Since that time, every year, on the 8th of September, the Fiesta of the Virgin of the Pines is celebrated and numerous pilgrims from all over the island come to Teror to pay reverence to the saint.

The beautiful Basilica de la Virgin del Pino, the church in the centre of the town, contains the 15th century carving of the Virgin and is suitably adorned. The day itself is a day of pilgrimage and many islanders, as well as visitors, walk to the town from all over the island as many believe that the Virgin has healing powers. This fiesta is not only the biggest event in the region – it is also the most important religious festival on the island's calendar and the celebrations usually go on for one week, as do the parties!

Just a few words of advice, if you do decide to visit the town it is best not to take a car with you if you wish to retain complete windscreens! When we first arrived on the island, we tried to visit the town during the week of this fiesta only to be met by groups of town vigilantes insisting that we park our car in their field, rear garden, patio or whatever at hugely inflated prices. As these hooligans were brandishing sticks and clubs at anyone who tried to park without their blessing we hastily drove away. Indeed, it was less than a warm and spiritual welcome to the town of the Virgin and the Pines!

BARRIE MAHONEY

The Canary Islander

Health

The Boob Job

Ladies, have you ever thought about breast enlargement? Gentlemen, have you ever considered having your 'man boobs' removed or maybe 'levelled off' a little? How about a 'nip and tuck' or maybe teeth implants or eye surgery? Well, you will be pleased to know that in the Canary Islands we can offer all such delights and at a much lower price than in the UK and many parts of Europe. In short, if it is hanging off, bulging, or not working as well as it did then we have specialists on hand here to help you!

It was only recently when I met Karen in one of the busy tourist bars in the south of the island a few days ago that I realised that the medical tourism business in the Canary Islands is growing so fast. Karen, a bride to be, with a six-year-old daughter, Shelly, from her previous marriage had always felt self conscious about her figure and she felt that she had reached the 'now or never' time of her life. When the new love of her like, Mike, finally popped the question, and they decided to get married, Karen decided that as a special treat to herself, as well as for Mike, she would have breast enlargement surgery.

After considerable research and recommendation, Karen came on holiday with Mike and Shelly to Gran Canaria to have her operation in one of the private hospitals. As part of the package, she was accommodated in one of the five star hotels close to the hospital. Karen told me that she received wonderful treatment and excellent post-operative care, as well as the ideal conditions for recovery. Mike and Shelly flew back to the UK the week after Karen's operation, allowing Karen a further week on the island for recuperation.

A new pair of breasts seems a strange souvenir to take back from holiday, but Karen assured me that she would do it again if she needed any other kind of cosmetic surgery. Hospital superbugs are virtually non-existent in the Canary Islands, and the cost of treatment is up to 40% less than other UK and European medical tourism destinations, even with the current exchange rate. These benefits, combined with the fact there are no waiting lists, appear to make the Canary Islands an ideal destination to meet medical needs safely and in a superb location for recovery.

As I bought Karen another drink, I asked her if it was really Mike that had persuaded her to have the operation. Karen dismissed the suggestion and assured me that it was all her own idea and that Mike was now considering having his man boobs reduced. "It's either that or a honeymoon cruise," sighed Karen.

Personally, I am quite happy to resist the temptation of assessing the various qualities of ladies' breasts, because there are greater experts than I. However, I thought Karen looked confident, fabulous and indeed beautifully proportioned. Indeed, I am happy to reassure readers that there would be absolutely no question of Karen drowning should she fall overboard during her honeymoon cruise!

A Playground for the Wrinklies

I have always liked the small Canarian coastal town of Arinaga, situated on the eastern side of the island of Gran Canaria. Unlike the sun-drenched tourist beaches of the south, Arinaga tends to attract a hardier type of holiday-maker and resident who shun the expense and crowded beaches of the south in favour of a calmer, more genuine Canarian seaside environment. True, despite the magnificent bay, the beach itself boasts grey sand rather than the white or golden variety, but at least it is natural and hasn't been imported from the Caribbean! However, the promenade more than makes up for any deficiency with its rich variety of restaurants and bars - just right for enjoying a bracing walk. I say bracing, because this must be one of the windiest parts of the island. However, for those of us who have tolerated a miserable few hours in the heat of the summer in the baking heat of Puerto Rico - this breath of fresh sea air comes as considerable relief.

The only thing I don't like about Arinaga, and the main reason why I could never stay there for long, are the lamp-posts that follow the length of the promenade and bend dramatically towards the sea! Even the lifeguard lookout station leans at a frightening angle! I have no doubt some renowned architect or town planner thought it a good wheeze, but as someone who likes tidy, straight lines I personally find it highly disturbing and wish they hadn't bothered! Homage to the sea can be demonstrated in so many other less-challenging ways! Maybe it is the same reason why the Leaning Tower of Pisa does absolutely nothing for me and, in my opinion, would be better knocked down and rebuilt - and this time vertically!

Since arriving in Gran Canaria, I have been fascinated and impressed by the politics of the small municipality of Aguimes, of which Arinaga is part. Locals tell me that, in the time of General Franco, Aguimes was one of the few municipalities in the islands to put two fingers up to the fascist dictatorship in Madrid, and continued with their fiestas and other celebrations as normal. These flamboyant events had been generally banned by the General and his regime at the time - but this was totally contrary to the Canarian spirit. By all accounts, this local opposition was mostly ignored and the locals were able to get on with their fiestas as normal. The group in power in the Town Hall at the time were mostly young idealists of communist/left wing socialist persuasion and it is these young "firebrands" of yesterday who continue to advise and mentor the new generation of politicians in the municipality.

Aguimes continues to take its social responsibilities very seriously. It is one of the municipalities that takes its concern for single parents, women alone at home, elderly people, the disadvantaged and the education of the young very seriously. One example of this concern can be seen during a walk along the impressive promenade at Arinaga. Here you will find an assortment of machines that would not look out of place in a well-equipped gymnasium. After initially thinking that these were modern equivalents of playground equipment for children, I noticed a sign that indicated that the equipment was not to be used by anyone under the age 15. Further investigation revealed that this equipment was intended for use by adults. Stepping machines, machines to strengthen legs, arms and all parts of the body were there for anyone to use - and completely free of charge.

I noticed two elderly woman taking advantage of these facilities. One had great difficulty walking, yet was using one of the machines to gently exercise. Another was tugging at the machine that would help to strengthen arm muscles. Both women seemed quite content exercising and chatting whilst enjoying the sea view. Where else would we find facilities of this kind so freely available and in such a wonderful setting? Well done, Aguimes and Arinaga! I hope your very local brand of politics, with people and their needs at the very heart of what you are trying to achieve, continues successfully for many years to come.

A Question of Convenience

One of my favourite stores in Spain and the Canary Islands is El Corte Ingles. This chain of stores is a combination of the UK's House of Fraser and John Lewis department stores, with a Spanish flavour thrown in for good measure. Prices may be a little on the high side, but customer service is generally very good and, a real plus point, they have toilets that are free to use! This is a real bonus in a country where public conveniences are not the norm. Indeed, although bars are obliged by law to make their facilities available to non-customers, I find that I cannot use them without ordering a drink and so the whole process starts once again. Yes, El Corte Ingles breaks this vicious cycle of events and provides considerable relief to many!

A few days ago, it was heart warming to hear a conversation between a father and his small son in the washrooms of El Corte Ingles. Father was insistent that his small son washed his hands with soap and water and after inspecting them he reprimanded the small boy for not doing so thoroughly and made him repeat the process. This, the small boy did, although he failed to put his paper towel in the bin. Again, the father made the small boy pick up the paper towel and place it correctly in the rubbish bin. This made a pleasant change from the increasing trend for men not to wash their hands after using urinals and, horror upon horrors, not even washing their hands after using the cubicles. No doubt they then go on to have a coffee and croissant in the bar! This reminds me of recent research relating to the analysis of bowls of peanuts left on the bar for customers to dip into, but I won't go into this horror story here!

Most of us have some regrets in life, and this incident in El Corte Ingles reminded me of one that still haunts me from when I was the head teacher of a large primary school. It was in the days when we were all given our own school budgets to manage. After one particularly irritating school governor made the comment at a meeting that, in his view, we were using an excessive amount of paper towels and toilet rolls. We had a drive to reduce budget expenditure on cleaning materials. Questions were asked and after much analysing of computer print-outs and soul searching we discovered that, yes, it was true, we were spending far too much upon these disposable items. So much so, as the school governor pointed out to me with great glee, we could afford to appoint one 40th of a class teacher if we reduced this spending. I pointed out that, appointing one 40th of a teacher or not, hands still needed to be washed and bottoms wiped, but to no avail...

The result was the installation of hot air hand-driers. Now, in those days, this really was high tech stuff and I looked proudly on as the gleaming white boxes were carefully installed on the walls of the toilets, at appropriate child height, with great satisfaction. Yes, it was true that for the next few days, infant pupils kept disappearing to the toilets to "wash their hands", but, I reasoned incorrectly, this novelty attraction would soon wear off. Sadly, this was not to be the case and it was during one of my patrols that I discovered a small boy alone in the toilets during lesson time, standing on an upturned plastic milk crate with his bare bottom placed strategically a few centimetres away from the hot air blower! The poor boy had wet himself in class and, full marks for initiative, thought that this would be the best way to overcome his embarrassment.

I soon discovered that hot air hand driers never really work - not for small children anyway. They are in far too much of a hurry to get on with life. After the initial novelty, it was clear that children either did not bother to wash their hands at all, or left the toilets with hands dripping wet, resulting in chapped hands during the bitterly cold weather of winter time. It was a great mistake and if I ever see that particular school governor again, I shall have great pleasure in telling him so. Oh, and the small boy's name? I kid you not, it was Jeremy Rowbottom!

"We love the NHS!"

Last year loud voices were raised on each side of the Atlantic concerning the best way of providing a health service that is based upon need and not the ability to pay. The raucous screeches of the Republican far right were unusually successful in creating an unholy alliance between the UK political parties, mostly stoutly defending the UK Health Service and the principles of its founders. Surprisingly, the issue appears to have, for once, united the views of the previous UK Prime Minister, Gordon Brown and the previous Leader of the Opposition, David Cameron, with each posting their comments on the "We Love the NHS" Twitter site.

There were a number of frightening statistics quoted in the press during that period. Yes, I know that statistics can be manipulated to say almost anything, but the claims that around 27 million people in the USA have insufficient medical cover and that a further 48 million people have no medical cover at all are, if true, very worrying. How can this be in one of the richest economies on the planet?

It is easy to forget in this debate that the National Health Service is no longer unique to the UK. Similar, broadly based services are in operation throughout Europe - as the many tourists to these destinations each year will testify. I know many expats living in the Canary Islands who have benefited from the excellent Spanish health service successfully treating serious conditions such as heart attacks, brain surgery and strokes - services freely given, based upon medical need and not the ability to pay.

I remember when living in the Costa Blanca talking to Robert, one of our neighbours and a good friend. Like us, he moved to Spain to start a new life in the sun. However, Robert's dreams were to be cut cruelly short just as he and his wife were purchasing their new dream villa. Robert was diagnosed with terminal cancer and his doctors in the UK gave Robert just a few months to live - and with a much reduced quality of life. Robert and his wife still moved to Spain and set about living their dream, albeit with this devastating nightmare hovering around them, knowing full well that their time together in their dream home was shortly to come to an end.

Robert went to see doctors in the Costa Blanca, where he was given a number of tests. Eventually, the Spanish specialists came to broadly the same conclusions as their counterparts in the UK. However, instead of giving Robert only a few more weeks to live, Robert's Spanish consultants prescribed drugs and care that would not only enhance his quality of life, but also to extend it. This was treatment that was not made available to Robert in the UK. Robert lived for a further two years, relatively discomfort free and gave him a quality of life that he thought had been denied him. Until the day he died, Robert was continually full of praise for the Spanish health service - a service that he had received totally free of charge, under the reciprocal agreements with the UK.

Surely, it is the cornerstone of any caring, compassionate and civilised society that the poor, elderly and needy are cared for and that the sick are treated, not according to their ability to pay, but based upon their medical needs. I applaud President Obama for honouring his election promise to bring affordable health care to all sections of the American public, and not just those with fat bank balances and expensive insurance policies.

Legal and Financial

Whack a Banker!

The human race has always enjoyed finding a minority to persecute. Whether it is the colour of skin, sexuality or religion, we always manage to find a convenient scapegoat for grievances, and particularly during the bad times. A recent UK survey of 'people's worth to society' concluded that bankers are a drain on the country, because of the damage they caused to the global economy. It certainly appears that bankers are the new persecuted people...

Have you heard of the new, very popular, and delightfully named, arcade game called 'Whack a Banker'. Apparently, it is all the rage in the UK and involves whacking bankers on the head with a wooden mallet. These are not real bankers, I hasten to add, but plastic, bald, faceless 'lookalikes that pop on a board ready for the player to bash them on the head with a wooden mallet. Punters pay 40p a time to hit as many bankers as they can in 30 seconds. When a customer wins, a voice says: "You win. We retire. Thank you very much to the taxpayer for paying our pensions." Hmm, now there's an idea...

So, will this delightful game take off in Spain? I suspect it might if a suitably modified language version becomes available. Just as with banks in the UK, Spanish banks vary in their approach, flexibility and quality of service to their customers. However, one thing that they do have in common is their general lack of customer service. When I arrived in Spain, I quickly learned that in most, but not all banks, customers should be prepared for a long wait, taking a flask of coffee and sandwiches if necessary, in order to stand in a queue awaiting their turn for a good half morning. In most banks the one and only cashier struggles to carry out the simplest, as well as the most complex, of transactions, answering endless queries, as well as ever intrusive telephone calls - both mobile and fixed (bank as well as personal). I can never understand this because invariably the branch appears to be full of non-engaged staff either chatting to each other, engaged in non-essential tasks or having a cigarette break outside the front door. Maybe a little flexibility is in order here; for example, if a non-engaged member of staff sees a lengthy queue, maybe they could help out? Simple stuff, eh?

I can never understand why the telephone has priority over the customer, patiently waiting for their turn. Surely if we have been waiting in the bank for an hour or so, we should be the priority over the customer who calls on a whim, asking for an account balance and whose query is answered immediately?

In general, I have found that the savings and local banks, similar in their mutual constitution status to the UK building societies, have a much greater understanding of their customers' needs than the large countrywide institutions that appear to hold the nation's financial cards. They have no shareholders and the good ones actually put money back into charitable causes, as well as the local community. Now there's a good idea for UK bankers. Maybe, if they did more of this instead of looking to their bonuses, they wouldn't be disliked (and whacked) quite so much.

Until death do us part (or until someone better comes along)

Recent divorce statistics from Spain's National Statistics Office are, at first glance, alarming. The figures show that in the Canary Islands the rate of 3 divorces per thousand of the population is the highest in Spain, where the divorce rate has fallen by 10 per cent since the time of the last survey in 2008.

Given that, for many, these islands appear to be an island paradise that draws many Northern Europeans to the islands, begs the question "What has gone wrong for these couples?" I can only guess that most of these breakdowns will be in the younger age group and are linked to the stresses caused by a lack of jobs, homes and a bleak future.

It is traditional for Canarians to marry when they are young. Many are still not out of their teenage years when the pressures of many overbearing families, and a mostly symbolic Church, forces them to take their wedding vows. It is not unusual to see, what appears at first, to be a brother and sister taking a baby out in the pram or playing with a toddler on the beach. It is only when chatting to these 'brothers and sisters' that we discover that they are in fact husband and wife and that the child is their own.

Needless to say, many of these young couples do not have the financial resources to rent a flat or to start a mortgage and, as a consequence, they are forced to live with their in-laws. This brings its own pressures on any couple. In the past, this has meant that grandmother has taken on the burden of raising the child and later providing after-school care, whilst the young parents are able to finish their education or start a career, but times have changed. The pressures of living within an extended family for far longer than in the past, and the inability of obtaining a home of their own, places unbearable pressures upon many families.

The problems have become more acute in recent years with the influx of expats moving to these islands. The best and most affordable properties have been snapped up by expats, forcing house prices, goods and services to increase as a consequence. It is an anomaly that despite the popularity of these islands as a holiday destination, they remain the bastions of unemployment, low pay, long hours and a reliance on 'black money' rather than secure contracts offering a living wage to local people.

The islands' government has attempted in recent years to provide affordable housing for young families, but the supply and availability of such properties has been slow and requires a steady income, which many young couples do not have. As many of us will remember from the UK, affordable housing, starter homes and other such well-meaning schemes do not remain affordable housing for very long.

We are often told that Spain is a very family-orientated society, and so it is - far more than many would consider realistic or desirable in the UK. In Spain, it is customary for all members of the family to take responsibility for, and to look after, the young, elderly and sick members of their family. In the Costas and the Canary Islands, residential homes for the elderly are few, with the exception of several run by nuns for the elderly with no families.

Island living, although idyllic in many ways, also brings other pressures that are often not realised. Island living often creates, by definition, an insular view of life. Despite attempts by schools to widen their pupils' experiences, many have never left these islands. Whereas school leavers in Peninsular Spain and other parts of Europe attend universities far from home, gaining rich experiences and meeting a wide variety of other people, as they complete their formal education, many Canarians study locally and have never left the islands. I recall putting the question of travel to Peninsular Spain and further afield to one young Canarian in his thirties. His reply was, "Why should we? We have everything that we need here." However, it is this insularity of knowing maybe only the people that we went to school with, or those from the same town or village that creates its own problems.

Hopefully, these recent statistics will provide opportunities for some soul-searching amongst clerics, local and national politicians. The statistics will also provide useful fodder for university researchers and the like. Hopefully, society too will look seriously at the pressures that young Canarian families currently face and take action. However, in these days of recession and financial cutbacks, I somehow doubt that anything positive will happen to address an obvious problem.

The Telemarketing Plague

Do you receive endless email spam messages advertising all kinds of competitions, pills and potions and, in particular, Viagra? The Viagra ones are particularly sinister, I find. After all, do they know something that I don't? They are, of course, easily dealt with by using the delete button, and some email providers also provide very sophisticated software that will weed out some of the most annoying and offensive messages and blast them into the ether. Sadly, it is a fact of modern day living that most of us are bombarded with all kinds of advertising, junk mail and unwanted phone calls.

The Spanish love their mobile telephones and it is customary for all businesses, Government offices, banks and services to ask for a mobile telephone number. I realised long ago that this was mainly a ploy to sell future services and, as a result, I usually give an old mobile number that I never answer anyway. However, it is the endless and uninvited calls to my new mobile phone, when I have only given that number to family and friends that I find most annoying.

This morning we received a total of four uninvited calls to our two mobile phones, as well as the home line, and that was before coffee! Be it the beast Telefonica, Movistar, Vodafone or Orange, the result is always the same. After a few weeks with a new mobile or landline number, the calls begin. These calls used to be mainly to tempt us away from one phone operator to another by offering an additional service or a special offer, some of which were quite useful. Now, I find that these numbers are sold on, and most calls are now advertising lotteries, asking me to take part in a 'survey' of some kind, offering a range of financial and insurance services, as well as some offers of a very doubtful nature. Not only are these calls annoying, but also they can be very distracting when working or driving. These calls must be a particular problem for the elderly or sick, particularly when received very late in the evening.

I always used to answer my mobile phone in Spanish. This, I thought, was the very least I should do when living in Spain. However, I would find myself drawn into an endless and confusing conversation about various products and services that I had no intention of buying or had the time to listen to. I am also well aware of the number of sales people who are desperate to make a living and earn a very tiny income from such calls. Somehow, it also seemed impolite to cut off the caller and I have, in the past, tried to be patient and courteous with them.

My attitude has now changed. Whenever I receive a mobile phone call, I now always answer in English. There is usually a brief pause and as soon as the caller realises that I am not Spanish, or unwilling to speak in Spanish, they cut off. Problem sorted!

Sadly, my new approach has still has not solved the problem of the phones ringing late into the night and, short of switching them off, there must be another way. I have tried calling the mobile operators requesting that my numbers be removed from their calling lists and their unbelievable response was that "it is not possible to do this in Spain". Unlike the 'Mailing Preference Service' for post and the ease with which such telephone calls can be blocked in the UK, this seems to be a real omission in consumer rights in Spain. If anyone does know how to block these endless calls, do please let me know!

The Parking Ticket

Last week I received a denuncia. Yes, the very word, 'denuncia' tends to strike fear in the very soul of the newly arrived expat living in Spain, but I have been around long enough to know that it only means 'police report' and, in my case, 'a parking ticket'. Even so, it was not pleasant to receive; such a nasty shade of yellow - cheap quality paper too, rather like the tortuous Izal toilet paper of my childhood, and stuck to the windscreen of my beloved Suzuki. My crime? Well, I had committed that most heinous of crimes - parking Suzy in an area where I was not supposed to park - despite there being no signs or lines telling me not to do so. What was even more annoying was that there were many other cars parked in the same road as well - but only Suzy had a ticket. Maybe she just exudes 'Brit Abroad'!

Trying to be a good citizen, I felt it my duty, two days later, to make the trip to the Town Hall to be absolved of my sins. Being well aware of the Spanish love of documents, I had the foresight to take with me my passport and residencia - originals not copies. You see, like so many, I have been caught out on that one before! I also took the documentation for the Suzuki, insurance documents, local tax documents and even my inside leg measurements, just to be on the safe side! You just never know what local officials will insist upon - many like to send you home, having to return with that elusive piece of paper another day.

Eventually, I managed to find the ticket machine for the queue and realised that something to do with 'multa' seemed to fit the bill. I joined the lengthy queue of criminals ready to plead for penance and hand over their fines. There were forty or so other miscreants in front of me and I began to wonder if the warning from a hardened expat when I first arrived in Spain was true. "Watch out for parking tickets and fines just before Christmas. They try to get extra money in for their Christmas party..." Certainly, the length of the queue indicated that this year's Christmas party was going to be a very good one indeed.

Eventually, two hours later, with my blood pressure far higher than when I had arrived, I sat at a grey table opposite an equally grey, wizened and thoroughly depressing official. Without a word, he took my shabby yellow piece of paper, peered intently into a computer for several minutes, grabbed my residencia document and then disappeared. A few minutes later he returned, clipping a copy to his newly printed documents, applied the obligatory 'bonk' of the rubber stamp and sat back in his chair. I asked how much it would be. With a smirk, he told be it would be one hundred and eighty euros, but that as I had been a good person in applying for forgiveness early it would be discounted to 90 euros. That was double what I had expected. I offered him my credit card in payment, but I was merely waved over to another equally long queue in another room.

This was another depressing and thoroughly irritating experience. The queue snaked around the room and out of the door. At the side of the cashiers' office was a branch of a well-known bank, together with a cash machine - all obviously essential if the fine means that you need a personal loan or mortgage to pay it. An hour or so later, I eventually presented the sheet of my now disintegrating 'toilet paper' to yet another unsmiling, equally wizened, clerk. After demanding my residencia and passport, she grabbed the credit card and ran it through her machine. She paused and glared at me.

"British?" she asked. I nodded.

"That'll do nicely", she replied, with the first smile of the morning.

Be warned, if the size of the fine doesn't hurt you, then your patience and possibly your pride after a morning at the Town Hall certainly will. I came to the conclusion that the misery inflicted at the Town Hall is part of the punishment process and that, if there is a next time, I will be better prepared. If you are ever unfortunate enough to have to follow in my footsteps, I advise you to take a flask of coffee, some sandwiches and a picnic chair!

Police Crackdown on Speeding Infants

I never cease to be amazed by the total lack of road sense shown by some drivers in Spain. No, I am not just talking about Spanish and other European drivers because, I understand from reliable sources, that it is more often than not the Brits who are responsible for many of the road accidents over here. After all, it is still not unusual to see British drivers driving the wrong way around a roundabout or speeding down a one-way street in the wrong direction. It's all very well complaining that, "These Europeans drive on the wrong side of the road," but I doubt that argument is a sound defence in court.

In our village it is not unusual to see a toddler sitting on his father's lap driving the family car around the village. At first I used to think it was very tiny men driving the cars, but once I had my new glasses I could see exactly who was really driving; my discovery was very worrying! I regularly see many a confident two-year-old confidently grasping the steering wheel of the car, whilst peering over the dashboard, whilst father proudly operates the clutch and, I hope, the brake.

The Christmas and Kings' Day festivities bring with them a new tranche of expensive gifts for many over-indulged children. For the last two years there have been an ever-increasing number of micro motorbikes and tiny four-wheeled vehicles, especially designed for the seven-year-old who intends to have everything, available in shops and large superstores. Advertised as "a snip at five hundred euros" these 'toys' are indeed generous gifts, and which many children are more than happy to receive!

Christmas Day and Kings' Day is when these lucky infants, and their proud fathers, are anxious to try out their new roadsters for the first time. Although these micro bikes and mini four-wheel drive vehicles are tiny, they are packed with a considerable amount of punch, with many having a petrol engine capacity that would make a Black and Decker hedge trimmer feel envious! However, instead of taking them to the park, a disused airfield or scrub land, these micro infants bomb around the local village streets as if there is no tomorrow and some, according to many irritated neighbours, may well find that they have their early days of motorised transport suddenly sabotaged by randomly strewn packets of tin tacks! These irritating little vehicles, with engines that sound very much like swarms of constipated wasps, buzz, wail and whine from mid-morning until late evening. Thankfully, these tiny vehicles eventually run out of petrol or the battery runs down and both the vehicle and the infant are at last hauled home by their now despondent fathers.

The increasing trend for these tiny vehicles and their infant drivers to use public roads and pathways is worrying, and the consequences potentially lethal. Many local drivers are not careful and considerate road users. These tiny vehicles are not intended for road use and as such give poor protection against injury. It is very rare to see helmets worn and the issues concerning insurance and the protection of pedestrians is a minefield.

However, all is not lost. I am pleased to report that whilst driving out of the village yesterday I saw two police officers apprehend an unaware infant speeding in their direction on his brand new micro four-wheel drive (with father clinging on the back for good measure). The speeding infant was stopped just as he approached the main roundabout outside our village. The small boy, whom I doubt was much older than seven years, and his embarrassed father were in the process of being given a good talking to by one of the less than amused gentleman in green; the infamous yellow documents were already in the process of being filled in.

Be warned, motorised infants! I doubt that many seven-year-olds will have a denuncia for a Kings' Day present from the police!

BARRIE MAHONEY

Attitudes

Build 'Em Up and Knock 'Em Down!

A conversation with some friends visiting the Canary Islands from the States a few evenings ago made me think. "Why is it that you Brits build folk up and knock 'em down again so quickly?" was the question.

The comment was made in the aftermath of Cleggmania that swept Britain for a couple of weeks during the recent General Election campaign. Nick Clegg, an essentially unheard of leader of a relatively minor political party in the UK was suddenly swept into the public gaze during the televised debates of the three political leaders and the public liked what they saw, or so it seemed. Interviews, chat shows and the full glare of media attention was poured into questions such as the best sex that Nick had ever had, his shoe size and what he liked eating for breakfast. The fact that he has a Spanish wife and was rather fond of Europe didn't go down too well with the Eurosceptics, but it did propel Nick Clegg into the Hall of Fame - as far as the tabloids were concerned anyway.

As the dust is settling, Cleggmania has evaporated and the poor man is now being vilified in the tabloids. The question from my friends from the States has once again entered my mind and, yes, they do seem to have a point about the Brits.

As much as I love my fellow countrymen and women and a county of which I am still very proud to have as my heritage, it is an unfortunate trait of the Brits, in general, to build people up and then to take great delight in knocking them down. You have only to think of Fergie, Princess Diana, David Beckham, Tony Blair, Jonny Wilkinson, Katie Price, Susan Boyle ...the list is endless, to see what my American friends meant. For a time these people are treated like heroes, they become almost God-like in the public eye, only to have scorn poured upon them and be vilified by the tabloids shortly afterwards.

My contact with Spanish, German and, indeed, people from many nationalities on the island, leads me to believe that this is an unfortunate trait in the British as a race. Maybe it is a gene thing or maybe, as an island people, the days of Empire still have a considerable bearing upon our collective national psyche. Maybe we resent change, have become too cynical and resent the success of others.

Taking the argument once step further, I remember many of my friends and acquaintances over the years who have had the inspiration and courage to start their own businesses. No easy task for anyone in this day and age, I know. I remember initial comments ranging from "I doubt it will succeed," or maybe "Good idea, but it won't work" or if the business is successful, I hear grudging comments such as "He's just been lucky..." Believe me, experience tells me that there is no such thing as luck - you make your own 'luck' in this world.

Even more depressing are the comments that I hear if the business has failed. "I knew it wouldn't work" or "John just hasn't got what it takes..." I could go on and yet I am quite sure that most of us have heard very similar comments.

Contrast this to the attitudes across the Atlantic. Would-be entrepreneurs, people with ideas and the spirit of 'get up and go' to get something done are applauded and, in the main, encouraged. True, businesses and enterprises also fail there, but would-be entrepreneurs are applauded in the States for having tried even though they may have failed and not, as in the UK, despised and made fun of for having tried and failed. That is the great difference between our two cultures.

The British have rightly gained an enviable reputation throughout the world, developed and honed over many generations, for their sense of fair play, justice, fairness and empathy with others. Why is it then that this is such a major deficiency in the nation's character? Why is it that we love to build 'em up and knock 'em down? Maybe it just makes us feel that much better about ourselves.

The UK Election and the Euro Brit

As a confused teenager growing up in rural Lincolnshire, my mother always insisted that I refrain from talking about politics, religion, vegetarianism or sex at the dinner table. Three of these "no, no's" I was quite happy to avoid, but there was one that I never quite managed to avoid, and I will leave you to guess which one. In later life, I applied the same principles to many conversations - in polite company. Anyway, during the pre-election period in the UK, I will break this now self-imposed taboo and raise the question of Britain's place within a united Europe.

Why is it that the British, a tolerant, decent and principled people when at their best, are some of the worst when it comes to xenophobia, building people up and then taking great delight in knocking them down, and so cynical when it comes to the question of national and European politics? It continually amuses and amazes me that when speaking to expats living and working in Spain, and often the British seem to be the worst offenders, that many have little time for Europe. Indeed, they have little time for the country of their birth either, which is presumably one of the reasons why they are now living in Spain. Unequalled by any other nation, just gather a group of British expats together, mention Gordon Brown, and the tirade of abuse that floods from the lips of those who have not lived or worked in the UK for the last 20 years or so hits one's ears with a vengeance. Even David Cameron seems to take his own fair share of stick, particularly those who remember the divisive policies of Thatcher's 80s, and I doubt that the Lib Dems will be safe from voter abuse for very long either.

Since moving to Spain, I gave up my right to vote in UK elections long ago. During this election period, we are reminded that we can vote in the UK elections for up to 15 years after we leave the UK. Even after two years away from the UK, I felt that I no longer had the moral right to vote, but would become an amused and interested observer of UK 'goings on' within a European context. What interests me now is the political situation and social progress made in Spain where we now live and work. Surely this is more relevant to the expat living in Spain?

I recall speaking to a colleague in Spain some time ago. He had not lived or worked in the UK for nearly 30 years, having lived in South Africa for many years and left 'in a huff' when black South Africans took the responsibility for running their own country. He moved to Spain, but spent most of his time criticising the UK, which I could never understand because he left the UK when he was very young. Be it education, family values, motoring or immigration issues, he always had a negative, cynical view of what was happening in the UK. He also had very strong views against the South African government of which he was, and still is, vehemently opposed. However, not once have I heard him comment about Spanish politics, laws, government and political progress in the country that he has adopted as his own for the last fifteen years or so, and which has been very good to him. He is, in the true British tradition, quite happy to whinge, moan and criticise anything that he can - from a safe distance on his terrace in the sun. I wonder if this is a healthy pre-occupation?

I hope that no readers of this book come into this category, but if you do, I really would urge you to try to forget the vicious, neo-fascist ramblings of some of the UK tabloids and try to understand the politics, traditions, culture and language of the country that you now live in. It is not only about taking; it is about giving something back to our adopted country as well. Most of us living here have benefitted from the European dream by the very fact that we are freely living and working in Spain, so maybe a little understanding of the European Union ideal that made it possible would be a good idea as well.

Sorry Mum, but it had to be said. Yes, I will leave the table now and go to my room...

The Beautiful Game?

I have always hated sport. Yes, I've said it aloud at last and I feel much better for it! It stems from the days when I attended my grammar school in Lincolnshire. I still have nightmares about those cold, wet and interminably long Thursday afternoons on the rugby field wishing, begging and pleading for the game to be over for another week, and I could return inside to the warmth. There were just so many things that I did not understand. Why was the ball that stupid shape anyway? I could see the point of football, but we were neither allowed to mention, let alone play soccer from the moment that we arrived at that ghastly institution at the tender age of eleven until we managed to escape its clutches forever.

Maybe it had something to do with having to wear my brother's elderly rugby boots. I really do believe that Noah had this particular pair in a cupboard in the Ark - just waiting for one of the tribe to play rugby! By the time they were handed down to me they were real antiques and, my goodness, didn't the other boys let me know it! They were made from painfully strong, inflexible leather and how my feet hurt afterwards. What I would have given for a pair of modern Nikes! Most of all it was the weather. It was always cold, wet and foggy and how I wished I didn't have to be the hooker yet again!

However, I quickly learned escape tactics. Although I couldn't physically escape from the game, match or whatever it was called, unless I had yet another sick note from my mother, I did retreat into my own very special world. Daydream, make-believe or fantasy, whatever you like to call it, but it was a far better place to be and I spent much of my time there. This probably explains why I was always the last boy to be chosen for the team. Mind you, this world of my own special creation is still a wonderful place to be, and, now that I am a writer, it has proved to be invaluable resource. Maybe I did learn something from that place after all.

I now realise that the main reason that I hated sport so much was that I couldn't actually see the ball! Not very well anyway, and so maybe things would have been very different if that little problem had been corrected many years ago. Nevertheless, I suspect that I would always have daydreamed and my own special world was never very far away. Athletics, and javelin throwing in particular, were yet another issue of considerable concern. Readers may be relieved to know that teachers quickly realised that letting me loose with a javelin was not a good idea and forced me to 'put the shot' or 'shot the put' (I can never remember which it is) instead.

Over the last few weeks, my attitudes and opinions have gradually changed because of the World Cup. I have seen the pleasure, involvement and excitement of local Spanish and Canarian people, as well as people of all nationalities visiting the islands on holiday. It has brought welcome relief at a time when we all need a break from the recession, financial and work problems, politicians, corruption and all the usual things that plague our daily lives. I love to hear the cheers and groans from the bars as yet another goal or penalty followed by the crazy tooting of car horns, cheering, fireworks and tremendous camaraderie following the recent Spanish victories on the playing field.

Possibly, I am a reformed sports person and maybe I have finally changed my mind about football after watching the World Cup finals. I now realise that perhaps I should have given it a far better shot than I have so far. Maybe in a different time and place, I would have done. Even so, it doesn't change my mind about that sport of the Devil - cricket, but that's a story for another time!

Fancy a change of career?

"French Air Traffic Controllers on strike!" screamed the headlines of one UK newspaper that I picked up recently. So, hand on heart, do any of us really remember when these lovely people were not on strike and were actually working? I think maybe not.

For as long as I can remember, French air traffic controllers have always gone on strike. It is one of the things that the French do best. After all, the concept is as much an intrinsic part of the French way of life, as eating fine food and farm subsidies. Sadly though, it happens at the most inconvenient of times, namely the summer months. It seems much like the 'British Disease' of the 70's and '80's when everyone seemed to be going on strike and hang the consequences for everyone else. Anyway, the fact that the French air traffic controllers are going on strike yet again seems to make little real difference to passengers this time, as recent arrivals to the Canary Islands confirmed, that they simply flew a different path instead. "The old expression, "Crying Wolf" springs to mind."

For tourists, heading to Spain's Costas and the Canary Islands this summer a far more serious dispute is looming. Passengers could face travel misery because of a row over Spanish air traffic controllers' pay. The Spanish government wants to slash salaries after it was revealed that some controllers are taking home an astronomical

£800,000 a year. Yes, you did read this correctly and it is not a typing error! This dispute could spark a "summer of discontent", with strikes and delays ruining holiday plans.

Although maybe not as noticeable as the French strikes, Spanish air traffic controllers have held many strikes over the past few years, causing travel problems for holidaymakers. Now, understandably, the Spanish Government wants to stop high wages and plans to slash more than £11 million off air traffic control costs. Recent statistics have shown that out of 2300 air traffic controllers employed by Spain's state operators AENA, 10 were paid between £725,000 and £800,000 last year - 10 times the salary of the Spanish Prime Minister. In Britain, the average wage of a controller is around £60,000, which may seem rather good to the rest of us.

Only a short time ago, passengers were hit by long delays because of staff shortages among controllers in the Canary Islands. Two runways were closed at Madrid Barajas airport recently for the same reason.

It is worth remembering that Spanish air traffic controllers caused heavy delays in 2002 and 2003 by striking. In 2003, they proposed 10 days of summer strikes because of a proposed change in the law they claimed would limit their rights. Regular travellers to Spain may well remember that in June 2002, hundreds of flights were cancelled after they ordered strikes to protest against unemployment benefit reforms. Maybe at a time of recession and the anger over bankers' bonuses they would do well to remember that no one is indispensable.

Boot-camps, (Arch)Bishops and Blogs

An item about a Chinese teenager who is now in a serious condition with chest and kidney problems after being beaten at a boot-camp caught my eye this week. This follows another incident where a fifteen-year-old was beaten to death in a similar 'treatment centre'. Their 'crimes', along with thousands of other teenagers across China, was 'being addicted to the Internet' and who are sent to 'boot style' camps across China to cure them of their addiction. Reports indicate that parents are willing to pay around £450 to have their teenagers 'cured' from playing too many on-line games, as well as the unforgivable sin of peering at the world outside China. A chilling quote from one of the 'therapists' responsible for setting up such camps is reported as saying, "Physical punishment is an effective way to educate children - as long as it can be controlled." With around 300 million Internet users, these boot camps are going to be kept busy controlling, punishing and torturing young Internet users for many years to come.

This article contrasted with, or maybe I should say was supplemented by, a recent article from Vincent Nicholas, the recently appointed Roman Catholic Archbishop of England and Wales, who took it upon himself to criticise social networking sites such as Facebook, MySpace and Twitter, as well as text messaging and emails as "undermining community life."

The Archbishop then went on to say that skills such as "reading a person's mood and body language were in decline", and that exclusive use of electronic information had a "dehumanising" effect upon community life. Apparently, social networking sites such as Facebook and MySpace are encouraging a form of communication that is not "rounded".

Well, there you have it. I thought, along with many other thousands of expats living in the Canary Islands and Spain, that using new technology in such a way that we can easily call and video-conference family and friends in the UK, send and receive text messages and renew friendships on social networking sites was actually enhancing family and community life. Obviously, I am completely wrong, and as it is such a heinous crime it is best stopped forthwith, if we are to avoid being sent to 'boot camps' in our thousands.

Oh, and to answer the Archbishop's comments, I cannot help thinking that if Jesus were around today he would be blogging, texting and 'Twittering' along with the rest of us!

People, Pets and Places

'From Teacher to Drag Queen'

My first novel, 'Journeys & Jigsaws Book 1: From Teacher to Drag Queen' finally hit the shelves of bookshops, and the warehouses of all the on-line bookstores. This novel had rather a long gestation period - it was about three years before that I first put pen to paper, or rather first hit the keys of my laptop in a hotel room in Fuerteventura. Pressure of work from the newspaper that I was editing at the time prevented me from writing much more for nearly two years. The novel was about many issues that had troubled me, and people like me, greatly during those often dark, sinister days of the 1980s.

Now it is finished, as is the sequel, and like all authors I enjoy responses from readers, but sometimes with some trepidation. One of the main questions that I have been asked by folk from the media or friends that I have not seen for some time, after the initial pleasantries, is "Barrie, are you a drag queen?" Let me try and answer this first question!

A drag queen is a unique performer and storyteller. Someone who can capture an audience and make them laugh, and maybe even cause them to be frightened or worried. A drag queen is someone who wears a very visible mask. Everyone knows there is a mask, yet everyone accepts that this is normal for the performance. Let me explain further, if you ever visit Las Palmas in Gran Canaria during Carnival you will find very few men, actually dressed as men - because most of the men are dressed as women! Everyone wears a costume and a mask and it just seems almost normal during that festival period. Indeed, you are very much out of place if you don't join in!

So as a writer, I hope that readers will be entertained. Many will laugh, be sad, frightened or may be worried when they read 'Journeys and Jigsaws', and certainly I hope that I will have challenged readers' preconceptions and views. So, if I have captured my audience in this way, perhaps I am a little like a drag queen! Maybe the short answer to this question is, no I am not a drag queen, but I am a great believer in career changes!

A Canarian Garden

Some of the few things that I miss from the UK are luscious green gardens, grass, flowers and trees. As the UK springtime approaches, I begin to crave for Cornish gardens with their snowdrops, bluebells, daffodils, camellias and all the wonderful plants and flowers that announce that springtime has finally arrived. All this is in such stark contrast to our small island off the Atlantic that basically has two seasons in the south, hot and very hot, whilst the more temperate north has a little more rain and cooler, cloudier days, which is more conducive to the growing of plants. In the south of the island, we have to content ourselves with a variety of palms, cactus and succulents that require very little moisture and can cope with soaring high temperatures and little rainfall.

In any case, I am not convinced that our Canarian neighbours would choose to garden, even if the temperature and rainfall were conducive to this very British of activities. Most appear content to lay patio tiles on any available patch of ground, with maybe the odd container plant that is rarely watered, shrivels up and dies within a few days of buying it from the small garden centres here - no tea rooms and greetings cards for sale in these garden centres, I'm afraid! There is a wonderful Botanical Garden in the north of the island, but I am not too sure how popular it is with local people, the few visitors that I usually see there are visitors to the island and not locals.

One of the first things that we did when we moved to our Canarian home was to install a watering system that switches on and off twice each day for just five minutes. This is similar to a wonderful system that one of our good friends and neighbours in the Costa Blanca insisted we install when we moved into our new home in Torrevieja. You would be surprised at the variety of plants that will grow even with this very small quantity of water. Even so, as I said earlier, this passion for gardening is not usual here - the outside living space being seen as an area for having family barbecues, as well as sitting and chatting with friends over a bottle of wine until the early hours of the morning. After all, gardening is such a waste of time and energy!

However, all is not lost. In the village where I live, there is a new housing estate. On one side there are the mountains and on the other there is the sea. In between and surrounding the estate is open, wasteland used for little more than exercising dogs and where some of the local teenagers choose to race their motorcycles. Ideally, this area should be planted with grass and trees, but this is not a viable option on these dry islands and so it remains an empty, unloved space.

Last year, whilst walking with my dog, Bella, I noticed that someone had marked out a piece of this wasteland near the footpath with large stones. Over the next few weeks more and more plants began to appear. Cactus, succulents and a whole manner of different plant life was planted and, what's more, were being watered. It was good to see, as I had suspected that this would be a short-lived wonder that would quickly be forgotten and the plants would be left to shrivel and die. Not so. Over the following months the plants flourished, and it was clear that someone was painstakingly watering them by hand with a bucket or watering can - and with no water supply nearby this is no mean achievement. Later, a small, home made, wooden garden seat appeared together with an old log and part of a wooden beer barrel.

Today, I walked past this garden again with Bella to find a small boy sitting on the garden seat. "He loves it here," remarked the young woman with the pushchair. "He likes looking at the plants." I asked if the young woman had created the garden and she shook her head. "No, I don't know who did it or who looks after it. It just appeared. What a pity there aren't more on this patch of land."

I agreed, and we both marvelled that the garden lay untouched by vandalism or litter for so long - created by someone who wanted to make something ordinary just a little bit better for all to enjoy. The wonderful thing is that further on my walk I noticed another row of stones marking out another new garden on the wasteland. Someone else is going to join in the fun!

Walking the Dog

Each day I take my dog, Bella, for a walk. We love her dearly, and inside our home she is a well-behaved, loveable and playful friend - in fact, a delightful and valued member of the family. As a puppy, she looked just like a tiny fruit bat and these distinctive features still remain. She is loyal, inquisitive and likes to be at the centre of all that is going on. During our holidays, when she goes off to kennels, she plays happily with other dogs and, we are told, that she is no trouble at all. However, it is a very different matter whenever we are out for a walk together, because she will growl and bark at any dog, cat or moving object that she sees. Dog experts tell us that this is because she is trying to protect us and, given her background as an abandoned puppy in the Costa Blanca, I tend to take their word for it.

I also still remember the trauma when Bella slipped her collar and went missing for several hours in Cartagena. As a result, she now wears a harness and I swore that I would never let her off her lead outside her home again. As a result if this deficiency in her all but perfect nature, Bella remains firmly at the end of a short lead on short walks, but we use a long extending lead on open spaces. She seems to be quite happy with the arrangement. At least we are well aware of the flaws in Bella's nature and take steps to ensure that she is safe, as well as ensuring that she does not annoy or inconvenience others.

One of the things that annoys and distresses me, both in the Costa Blanca as well as the Canaries, is the tendency for many Spanish families to let their dogs roam freely by day and then return home at night to eat and sleep. This used to be the traditional way, but with increased traffic, the rural idyll has all but disappeared in most neighbourhoods and many dogs and cats are the cause of road accidents. I had little sympathy with a neighbour whose dog was killed by a speeding car a few months ago. We have since noticed that the dead dog has now been replaced by another, who also roams the streets. The lesson has not been learned.

It is true to say that the dogs seem happy enough with the arrangement - roaming, playing and generally having a fabulous time with their mates. The downside is that many a playful encounter with the 'bitch across the road' leads to the distress of yet more unwanted and abandoned puppies and this is something that is taking time for the locals to fully grasp. Although neutering dogs and cats is promoted on the island, this is not always too successful, particularly during a recession when the costs are seen by many owners as being too high.

You can imagine the annoying scenario when walking Bella on a lead. Many an uncontrolled dog suddenly leaps forward to play with Bella. There is often no owner in sight resulting in a tussle between dogs wanting to play and Bella who does not. On several occasions I have had words of abuse, fortunately shouted in my direction in Spanish so I could not really understand the finer content of what was being said, telling me that I should let Bella run off a lead and then there would be no trouble. Hmm, that's what they think, but I tend to think that a few vital organs would go missing if I did!

A Cat and Dog Story

I have always been of the opinion that we are born as either golfers or dog walkers. Sorry, I can already hear some of you complaining, "But I play golf and I have a dog!" Well, maybe, but perhaps one takes clear precedence over the other? Personally, I am a dog walker and not a golfer. Maybe this is in much the same way that most people tend to prefer cats to dogs or dogs to cats. It's all about personal preference and, more often than not, whether we were brought up to love and respect animals during childhood, and whether we come from cat or dog families or maybe neither.

It was another hot, sunny day on the island and it was time for Bella's midday walk. Yes, I know all about "Mad Dogs and Englishmen and the Noonday Sun", but if Bella doesn't get her walk at lunchtime, then all hell breaks loose. So a very short walk it had to be. We walked over to the dry and dusty wasteland, after all it hadn't rained on the island since February, and Bella pulled with determination towards some old dry shrubs. In the UK it would have been called a hedge, but maybe that would be stretching the imagination too far over here. I tugged at her lead, assuming that she was on the hunt for yet another lizard, but she firmly refused to leave and stood her ground barking at whatever she had found beneath the dried out shrub. I knelt down and peered beneath and discovered what she had been barking at. It was a tiny bundle of matted, dirty white and grey fluff - a tiny kitten.

The tiny scrap of life hissed, growled and tried to scratch and bite, as I put my hand towards it and carefully lifted it out. Surprisingly, Bella, who usually hates cats, did nothing, but watched as I gathered up the poor little creature, wrapped it in my handkerchief and made our way home. The little kitten was only a few weeks old and not in a good state. It was very weak and clearly dehydrated from the baking heat, and I doubted that it would last the night. Still, I reasoned, at least we could make it comfortable during its last few hours.

We managed to buy a tin of cat food from the local shop and began to tempt the kitten with a teaspoon or so of the foul smelling contents of the tin. The kitten began to lick and then eat a little from the spoon and after a while hungrily devoured a tablespoon of so of the meat. He then lapsed into a deep sleep. We repeated the process again an hour or so later, and continued throughout the evening until the kitten could eat no more. Even so, by the time I went to bed, I doubted that the little thing would see morning.

Early the following morning, I peered anxiously into the old cage where we kept the kitten to see him standing and looking at me with enormous eyes. He hissed and growled, and tried to scratch as I picked him up. He ate several more large helpings of cat food during the day and was clearly recovering from his ordeal! Phone calls, Facebook, Twitters and emails to cat-loving friends brought us essential help and advice at a time when it was most needed. Thank you! We went out and bought the correct kitten food, cat litter, travel bag, scratch post and all the other necessities of life for the modern kitten. Adopting the kitten certainly gave the credit card a hammering!

As I write this Twitter, one week later, I am delighted to say that the vet has declared that Mac is a three-month-old boy. She thinks he is basically fit and well, although he has another examination next week, and has treated him for fleas, worms and diarrhoea! Even in this short space of time he is growing into a happy, contented, if nervous kitten that will happily spend his time on my knee purring and having his tummy and chin tickled. Thankfully, he no longer scratches, hisses or spits - at us anyway!

Mac will stay with us and has already become a much-loved member of the family. That is with the exception of Bella who, I fear, will regard the finding of Mac as the worst day's work that she has ever done in her life. Mac spends much of the day staring at her with big, threatening eyes and growls and hisses whenever she gets too close. I also suspect that it will be cat and not dog who will be in charge!

The Uniqueness of Gran Canaria

I often receive emails from readers asking why I moved from the UK to the Canary Islands, and to Gran Canaria in particular. In this 'Twitter' I will attempt to answer the question, but my apologies if it sounds as if I work for the Tourist Board. I don't, but I just happen to love the island!

Gran Canaria is often called a "continent in miniature". It is a fitting title because of the island's uniqueness of having several climatic zones within the one relatively small island. There can be snow on the mountains, whilst you are swimming in the sea or sweltering in the heat of the desert. In Gran Canaria, there are craters, volcanoes, waterfalls, mountains, pine woods, palm groves and beautiful sandy beaches making it a naturally stunning and interesting place to visit or to live. With its seemingly endless sandy beaches, dramatic mountains, deep ravines, sweeping sand dunes and lush green vegetation many have come to regard Gran Canaria as the jewel of the Canary Islands.

Whilst the north of the island frequently experiences dense, low cloud, often blocking out the sun for hours at a time; the southern coast of the island is perpetually cloud free and guaranteed rain free during eight months of the year, making it a popular destination for sun-seeking tourists. Average temperatures on the island are 24°C in summer and 19°C in winter. Unlike some of its neighbours, Gran Canaria has extremely varied landscapes with European, African and even American vegetation. There is hardly anywhere else in the world where you can find such differing landscapes and climate zones in such close proximity to each other.

What is the reason for this uniqueness of the island's climate? One of the reasons is the unusual shape of the island, which leads to a great variety of microclimates. While the climate is dry and sunny almost all year round in the coastal regions, particularly in the south, as you move up to higher altitudes, the influence of the sea is reduced and the clouds are retained by the mountains. This produces great variations in temperature from the temperate zones of the lower regions or valleys and subtropical forests to the highest zones where the temperature can fall to 0 °C. It's not too unusual for people to go sunbathing and swimming on the beach and then to find themselves playing around in the snow on the mountain tops just one hour's drive later.

The sea is equally as warm with temperatures fluctuating between 18 °C in the winter months and 22 °C during the rest of the year. This, together with the estimated annual rate of 2,700 hours of sunlight in Gran Canaria allow you to make the most of the day, whether you are on the beach, playing a sport, on a day trip or enjoying an outdoor activity.

People often mistakenly think that if the winter is so warm on the islands then the summer heat must be overwhelming, but this couldn't be further from the truth. The summer in the Canary Islands is softened by the trade winds that refresh the islands and give it mild summers. Indeed, one small village on the on the island's east coast, Pozo Izquierdo, is often said to be the "windiest place on earth" and there is rarely a shortage of a refreshing breeze. However, in the last couple of years there have been one or two weeks in August where the temperature has climbed higher than usual. As a bonus, research from the international scientific community claims that the island's capital, Las Palmas, is one of the cities with the healthiest climate in the world.

I could go on, but I am fast running out of space. All I can say is, come over and see for yourselves. You will be made most welcome!

LIVING THE DREAM

Made in the USA
Charleston, SC
03 October 2012